Jack O'Connell
Seattle
6 décembre 1982

THE BAYEUX TAPESTRY
AND THE NORMAN INVASION

the BAYEUX tapestry and the NORMAN invasion

With an Introduction and a translation from the
contemporary account of William of Poitiers by
LEWIS THORPE

LONDON

The Folio Society

1973

Fourth (litho) impression 1981

PRINTED IN GREAT BRITAIN

by Mackays of Chatham Ltd

contents

the historical background

In 1051 Edward the Confessor, King of the English, then aged about forty-eight, quarrelled with Earl Godwine and as a result dismissed Edith, his queen, who was Godwine's daughter. Edward had married Edith in 1045 at her father's instance, but in their six years together she had borne him no children. According to the chroniclers the marriage was never consummated.* When Godwine and his family returned to power in 1052 Edward took his wife back, but from 1051 until his death on 5 January 1066 there could have been no hope of a direct heir to the throne.

In 1036 Godwine had seized the person of Edward's brother, the Atheling Alfred, when he visited England from Normandy, and had handed him over to King Harold Harefoot's men, who had put out his eyes and occasioned his death. The immediate cause of the disagreement between Edward and Godwine in 1051 was the undue numbers and the excessive influence of foreigners, and especially of Normans, at the English court. Godwine, the son of Wulfnoth, was the leading Englishman of his time: he himself was Earl of the West Saxons, his daughter Edith was queen, his eldest son Sweyn already held an earldom in the west country and the Severn valley, and his second son Harold was Earl of the East Angles. On this issue of the favour which he showed to foreigners Godwine and his brood of sons prepared to offer armed resistance to the king, who was supported against them by Leofric, Earl of Mercia, and Siward, Earl of Northumbria; but in the end the whole family was outlawed, Godwine fleeing to Flanders and Harold finding refuge in Ireland in the company of yet another brother, Leofwine. Edward the Confessor, the elder son of King Ethelred II the Unready, was English on his father's side, but his mother was Emma, daughter of Richard I, Duke of Normandy. He had lived in Normandy as an exile for twenty-five years from 1016 until 1041, and he had very strong affiliations with the Duchy.

Long before Edward came to the English throne in 1042, the affairs of England and Normandy had been closely intertwined. William, Duke of

* *Vita Beati Edvardi Regis et Confessoris*, lines 203–216, Luard, p. 367.

Normandy, was known to have designs upon the English succession, and according to one authority, the *Anglo-Saxon Chronicle*, he is supposed to have visited King Edward in England in 1051. Whether this was true or not, his kinsman Edward, or so it was thought, in that year promised him the crown after his own death. As a result opinion veered back towards the outlawed Godwine, and later in 1052 he and his sons were able to return under arms to England. Robert of Jumièges, Archbishop of Canterbury, Ulf, Bishop of Dorchester, and a number of other Normans in high place were forced to flee the country in their turn. Sweyn died in 1052 and Godwine himself in 1053, but the power of Harold and his other brothers increased steadily from year to year. Harold himself succeeded his father as Earl of the West Saxons and, in 1055, on the death of Siward, Tosti, another brother, was made Earl of North-umbria. East Anglia was given to his brother Gyrth, and Leofwine held the south-east from Buckinghamshire to Kent. During the last thirteen years of Edward's reign Harold Godwineson virtually ruled over England.

As Harold's power in England grew ever greater, so from across the sea William gradually multiplied his own claims to the succession. William, 7th Duke of Normandy, although the illegitimate child of an artisan's daughter, was the grandson of Richard II, 4th Duke of Normandy, himself brother of that Emma who had been Edward the Confessor's mother: in short he was Edward's first cousin once removed. However interested their motives, William and his father, Robert I, 6th Duke of Normandy, had done many acts of kind-ness to Edward, and the King of the English owed them a great debt of grati-tude. In his successful campaigns against the rebels in the Bessin and the Cotentin in 1047, against William Busac, brother of Robert, Count of Eu, in 1048–53, against William of Arques in 1053, and against Geoffrey Martel, Count of Anjou, then allied with Henry I, King of France, in 1054 and 1058, William had established himself in Edward's mind and, indeed, in everyone else's, as a strong ruler and a most formidable fighting-man. In 1053 he married Matilda, daughter of Baldwin V, Count of Flanders, who traced her descent in the female line from Charlemagne and, what is more pertinent to the present argument, from Alfred the Great, Anglo-Saxon King of Wessex from 871–899. On the return of Godwine and his sons to England in 1052 and the conse-quent flight of Robert of Jumièges, Stigand, one-time chaplain to Canute and then Bishop of Winchester, was made Archbishop of Canterbury in Robert's place, and this defiance of canon law so alienated the Papacy that, when the moment of decision eventually came, Pope Alexander II was only too ready to issue a Bull which declared Harold a usurper and William the lawful claimant to the English throne. Stigand was excommunicated by five popes in succession. None of these arguments really affected the line of succession in England; but the fact that William believed that they did, and that he was able to persuade a vast number of other people to hold the same belief, was to be of the utmost importance when the time became ripe. As against all this, Harold Godwineson had no royal blood; but he was by birth and male descent an Englishman, he had shown great skill as an army commander in the Welsh wars against Gruffydd ap Llywelyn, King of Gwynedd and Powys, and he was all-powerful in England during the last dozen years or so of Edward's reign.

In 1063 or 1064 an event occurred which brought face to face the two eventual contestants for the English throne. For some reason which we shall never understand, possibly simply a pleasure trip in the Channel, Earl Harold set sail from Bosham with a considerable company in three ships (Tapestry 1–6). According to the two early Norman chroniclers, William of Jumièges and William of Poitiers, he was sent by King Edward to confirm formally and in public the promise of the succession to the English throne made to Duke William some twelve or thirteen years earlier. If this was so, one can only say that it is remarkable that Harold should have agreed to go on such a mission at a moment when he was at the very height of his power and of his expectations. He was caught in a storm and his ships were driven to the coast of Ponthieu, where he was captured by Guy, the local count, and locked up in the castle of Beaurain (Tapestry 7–10). The news soon reached William and he immediately ordered Guy to liberate his distinguished captive. Guy and Harold rode together to meet William at the castle of Eu, and there Harold became the guest of the Duke of Normandy (Tapestry 11–17). The two were still on friendly terms, although Harold's position as guest was clearly a most difficult one. Accounts of what happened differ in the various chronicles, but the wily William certainly took full advantage of the unexpected circumstances. Harold, who was some seven or eight years older than his host, is supposed to have promised to marry one of William's daughters, to have taken part with William in a military expedition against the Bretons (Tapestry 18–25), to have received knighthood from the duke's hands (Tapestry 25) and to have done homage to him, and then to have sworn an oath upon the relics of the saints that he would accept William as King of England after the death of Edward and in the meantime would do all in his power to bring this succession about (Tapestry 27). If he swore this oath one can only assume that he did so as one who, for all his appearance as an honoured guest, knew well that he was in reality a prisoner. Just where and when he swore is not known, some say Bonneville, some Bayeux, some Rouen, some even the manor of Bur; and the authorities for its ever having been sworn at all are all Norman. Whatever the circumstances and whatever the nature of the oath, it was to tell dearly against Harold in the minds of his enemies when the time came for William to embark with papal blessing upon a holy war against an alleged perjurer. After these adventures, all of them unfortunate, Harold was set free to sail back again to England (Tapestry 27–29).

In the last month of 1065 King Edward the Confessor lay dying at Westminster. This was common knowledge on both sides of the Channel. He was then some sixty-two years old and he had reigned over England since 1042. On Thorney Island beside the River Thames he had just completed the rebuilding of the great abbey church of Saint Peter in Westminster, a Benedictine house, although his illness prevented him from taking part in the ceremony of consecration on 28 December. The witenagemot* had gathered from all four quarters of England for the Christmas crown-wearing,† and one can imagine with what anxiety and sense of urgency its members had travelled to Westminster. For all his saintliness and the fact that he was so soon to be canonized by Pope Alexander III, Edward had been a poor king. Now his end was very near. Since 1052 he had been reconciled with the wife whom he had banished from his presence the previous year, and she sat weeping at his feet. At either side of his bed stood Stigand, Archbishop of Canterbury, and Harold, Earl of the West Saxons. There was also present Robert the Staller, Master of the King's Stables. Edward's only living blood-relations were his nephew and two nieces, the Atheling Edgar and Edgar's sisters, Margaret and Christina, the grandchildren of Edmund II Ironside, King of the English from 23 April until his death on 20 November 1016. Towards the end the dying king regained consciousness and rallied for a short time. 'He pointed with his hand towards Harold, the man

---

* The witenagemot or witan was the council of the Anglo-Saxon kings, consisting of such nobles, bishops, abbots, household officers and thegns as they cared to summon. It was convened whenever the kings wished. At Easter, Whitsun and Christmas it met ceremoniously.
† The king wore his crown in public at Easter, Whitsun and Christmas. The Norman kings continued this custom.

whom he had brought up at his court and whom he looked upon as a brother. "I commend my wife to your care", he said, "and with her my whole king-dom". '* He died almost immediately, on Thursday 5 January 1066 (Tapestry 31–32). The witan, which was already gathered, chose as Edward's successor Harold Godwineson, Earl of the West Saxons. The offer was made to him formally and he accepted the charge (Tapestry 32–33). On Friday 6 January 1066 Edward was buried in Westminster Abbey. On the same day Harold was crowned King of the English by Ealdred, Archbishop of York, and he made his three-fold oath to God and to his Christian people (Tapestry 33).

King Harold reigned for ten months only and during that short time he had much to occupy him. As the *Anglo-Saxon Chronicle* says in its quiet way: 'Earl Harold was now consecrated as king, but he found little peace in the realm as long as he ruled it'. According to the monk Florence of Worcester, all that he did was worthy of admiration. 'As soon as he took over the government of the kingdom, Harold set himself to rescind unjust laws, to replace them by just ones, to make himself the patron of churches and monasteries, to become the friend of bishops, abbots, monks and ordinary churchmen and to behave with due reverence towards them, to show himself pious, humble and friendly to all good-living men, and to be the enemy of all evil-doers. He gave orders to his leaders, local representatives and deputies, and to all his ministers without exception, that they should lay by the heels all thieves, highway robbers and disturbers of the peace, and that for the good of their fatherland they should make great efforts to achieve this, both on land and on sea.' The earldom of the West Saxons he kept in his own hands, for there was no-one to whom he could give it. A great amount of new coinage was struck, with, on the obverse, a crowned head facing left, with a beard, which Harold did not wear but which the moneyers had copied from Edward the Confessor. Harold gave new gifts to Waltham Abbey, which he had founded in 1060. He established or continued friendly relations with Gisa, Bishop of Wells, Leofric, Abbot of Peterborough, Aethelwig, Abbot of Evesham and, above all, Wulfstan, Bishop of Worcester.

Harold's immediate and pressing problem lay in the north. As was natural, given the season of the year and the conditions of travel of the time, the north had been sparsely represented at the witan which elected him as king. It is true that Ealdred, Archbishop of York, had placed the crown upon his head; but

* *Vita Ædwardi Regis*, lines 1561–1563, Luard, p. 433.

Edwin, Earl of Mercia, and Morcar, the new Earl of Northumbria, the two sons of Ælfgar, together with their Danish and Anglian adherents, could not be expected to take kindly to the rule of this West-Saxon king. The menace of Tosti, the new king's exiled brother, was ever in their minds, and in the mind of Harold, too. After the death of Siward in 1055, Tosti had been made Earl of Northumbria. His rule was strict and in 1065 his people rose against him. They declared him an outlaw, chose Morcar in his place and marched south as far as Northampton, where Harold came to meet them and perforce gave in to their demands. In 1051, during the exile of Godwine and his sons, Tosti had married Judith, daughter of Count Baldwin V of Flanders, thus being through his own sister brother-in-law of King Edward the Confessor and, two years later, becoming brother-in-law of William, Duke of Normandy, who married Matilda, Judith's sister. In 1065 he fled to Flanders and then to Normandy itself. Tosti thus became Harold's implacable enemy, and in his hands were soon to lie his brother's destiny and the eventual fate of all the men and women of England. Only too conscious as he was of all these hazards, Harold travelled to Northumbria, taking Bishop Wulfstan with him, and there, whatever the hidden feelings of Edwin and Morcar, he was received as King. In York he held a northern witenagemot, at which the people's allegiance was confirmed. At some time, probably during this visit to the north, he did what he could to placate Edwin and Morcar by marrying their sister Edith, widow of Gruffydd ap Llywelyn. He then returned to London and in April held his Easter witan and crown-wearing in Westminster.

It was at this moment that Halley's comet made its appearance and blazed its way across the night-sky from 24 to 30 April, a portent pregnant, it was felt, with dangers and disasters soon to come (Tapestry 34). According to Florence of Worcester: 'In this same year on 24 April the comet-star was seen, not only in England, but, or so they say, throughout the entire world, shining for seven days with great brightness'.

The news soon reached William of the death of Edward the Confessor, the election of Harold as his successor by the witan and the coronation of the new king in Westminster Abbey (Tapestry 35-36). He lost no time in sending envoys to Harold. The precise purport of their message is not known, but the essence of it must have been to remind Harold of his oath and to demand that he should surrender the crown of England which he had so recently received.

The terms of Harold's reply are reported differently by the chroniclers, but with-out doubt he refused point-blank. William could have expected nothing else, but, in his own mind, he had once again put Harold in the wrong.

From this moment onwards, and it was probably still January 1066, Duke William of Normandy devoted all his energies to the project nearest to his heart, that of the seizure of the throne of England by force of arms. He seems to have consulted Lanfranc, Prior of the Abbey of Bec and later to be Archbishop of Canterbury. The conclusion to which they came was that, of all the varied claims which William considered himself to possess, the two most convincing were Harold's failure to observe the oath which he was supposed to have made on the relics of the saints, and the severance of the Church in England from the Mother Church of Rome, in the two persons of Archbishop Stigand and Pope Alexander II. In short the planned invasion was to be a crusade, a holy war, and William would cross the Channel as the chosen representative of Christendom. William first called a select council of his known supporters, the great military leaders of the Duchy of Normandy, including his half-brother Odo, Bishop of Bayeux (Tapestry 36–37). Once assured of their support he convened a much wider assembly of Norman barons in the castle of Lillebonne. Here he met much opposition, but in the end he once again prevailed. His third move was to secure the backing of the other continental powers. If they did no more, the young Emperor Henry IV and his German supporters probably agreed not to hamper William. Sweyn Estrithson, King of Denmark, is supposed to have promised help, but in the end he preferred his cousin Harold. Neither Count Baldwin V of Flanders, nor Philip I, the young king of France, who was still under Baldwin's tutelage, showed much enthusiasm for the enterprise, but many individual Flemings and Frenchmen flocked to William's banner. Count Eustace of Boulogne, who had been insulted by Earl Godwine at Dover in 1051, was zealous in his support; and so were the men of Brittany. Most important of all, Pope Alexander II issued a Bull in William's favour, and sent a ring and a consecrated banner.

There remained the naval and military logistics of the campaign. Volunteers flocked to join William. Arms were prepared and supplies were assembled (Tapestry 40–41). The coast of Normandy stretches north-eastwards, from where the tiny Couesnon stream flows into the Baie du Mont Saint-Michel to where the River Bresle enters the sea at Le Tréport. All the harbours on this long coastline were in William's hands and they all pointed straight to England.

Farther to the north, the men of Ponthieu were his allies. His most pressing need was for transport-vessels. Vast numbers of these were built and vast numbers were requisitioned (Tapestry 37–39). The eventual strength of the fleet is not known and, in view of the variety of vessels used, this is not to be wondered at. '. . . I heard my father say,' wrote Robert Wace, 'and this I remember well, although I was only a lad at the time, that, when they set sail from Saint-Valery, counting boats, smaller vessels and skiffs carrying arms and armour, the fleet was 696 strong. I have read, and whether this is true or not I cannot say, that there were as many as 3000 vessels with their sails and masts.' By some time in August, troops, arms, horses and supplies were brought to-gether, Matilda and Roger of Beaumont had been put in charge of Normandy, and the invasion fleet was riding at anchor in the estuary of the River Dives.

When in 1065 Harold was forced to agree to the deposition and outlawing of his brother Tosti, Earl of Northumbria, the latter fled first to Flanders and then to the arch-enemy in Normandy. In May 1066 he came back across the Channel with a fleet of ships, harassed the Isle of Wight and attacked Sandwich. Harold, who with great energy was preparing his army and his fleet against the invasion which he knew must soon be launched from Normandy (Tapestry 34), had no choice but to interrupt these all-important affairs and march to Sandwich, but Tosti had already sailed away northwards. He entered the Humber and ravaged the coast of Lindsey. Driven off by the two northern Earls, Edwin and Morcar, he sought refuge with King Malcolm III of Scotland, with whom he stayed for several months. He next made his way to Sweyn Estrithson, King of Denmark, who refused to help him. From there he travelled even farther north and this time he was at length successful. Harold Hardraada, King of Norway, showed no interest in restoring Tosti to his lost Northumbrian earldom, but he was only too ready to lead an invasion of England which should have the object of deposing his namesake and making him king in Harold Godwineson's place.

Since the middle of August 1066 one vast invasion fleet had swung at anchor in the Dives estuary, less than a hundred miles from the English coast, while in the hidden folds of the nearby hills lay encamped an army of fighting-men of all ranks, fully equipped with arms, armour, horses and supplies, and lacking only one last boon, a breath of wind from the south. A second vast invasion fleet now moved out to the open sea, from Sognefjord, north of Bergen. According to Snorri Sturluson, Harold Hardraada had assembled some two hundred ships of war, not counting provision-ships and small craft, and in them he proposed to carry across the North Sea half the fighting-force of his whole kingdom.* William of Normandy must have had information of what the treachery of Tosti had achieved. It has been well said that when he landed on the pebbly shore of Pevensey Bay he could not have known whether it was Harold of England whom he would meet in battle, or Harold Hardraada, King of Norway.

The Norwegian fleet first made land in the Shetlands and Orkneys. From there Harold Hardraada sailed to the mouth of the River Tyne, where he was joined by Tosti. He ravaged the Cleveland coast from Tees to Esk, attacked Scarborough, plundered the shores of Holderness, sailed up the River Humber, and moved up its tributary, the Yorkshire Ouse, as far as Riccall, where his whole force landed, still without making naval or military contact with the two northern earls. York was in deadly and most imminent peril. Then at last Edwin and Morcar marched. The two armies met at Fulford Gate, two miles away from the northern capital, on 20 September. The English were beaten. Four days later York was invested, Northumbria accepted Harold Hardraada as its king and the Northumbrians agreed to march southwards with his army.

Caught between these two frightening invasions, the one a stark reality, the other a pressing and immediate threat, Harold had no recourse but to hasten north along the Roman road to York. Harold Hardraada had moved his camp to Stamford Bridge, on the River Derwent, some eight miles north-east of the city. At the head of his army Harold Godwineson passed through Tadcaster on 24 September, pressed on through York early the next morning, and met his enemies in battle at Stamford Bridge that same day, 25 September 1066, after a forced march of some two hundred miles and more. Harold Hardraada was killed. Tosti fell fighting beside him. The Norwegian army was annihilated and King Harold Godwineson won his finest victory, but the English losses must have been extreme. 'The site of the battle is obvious enough to all who travel in those parts', wrote Orderic Vital some seventy years later. 'To this day a great congeries of skeletons of those who died still lies there, as evidence of the whole-sale slaughter of two peoples.' His success at Stamford Bridge, which has been described as 'one of the most complete victories of the Middle Ages',† was to cost King Harold dear. Three days later William, Duke of Normandy, landed in Pevensey Bay.

* *Heimskringla, IX, Harald Hardraada, §§. 82–83.*
† D. C. Douglas, *William the Conqueror*, p. 194.

On 27 September the pennants at the Norman mastheads at last fluttered north-westwards, pointing the way to the open sea. Deus afflavit, but in an alien cause; now sat the wind fair, but for England, not for France. A fortnight earlier William had moved his invasion fleet from the River Dives to an anchorage off Saint-Valery, in the estuary of the River Somme. Some of his troops deserted and others were drowned in shipwreck, but these were trifling losses. The earthly remains of Saint Valerius of Luxeuil were paraded from his abbey, and the Norman soldiers passed their days in religious ceremonies and processions.

Once the long-awaited south wind began to blow, the invasion army lost no time in embarking and the ships put out to sea. Every vessel bore a light, and a great lantern shone from the masthead of William's own ship, the Mora. Once clear of land the fleet grouped together and dropped anchor. As the crow flies, Saint-Valery is some 65 miles only from Pevensey Bay, and it was no part of William's plan to strike land in the darkness.

The crossing is described in great detail by William of Poitiers (Tapestry 41–45). Later in the night a trumpet sounded from the Mora and its lantern gleamed bright: at this double signal the fleet weighed anchor and put out to sea. The Mora sailed faster than the other ships and when daylight dawned it had far outdistanced them. A man was sent aloft, but he could see nothing except the lonely sea and the sky. The Mora cast anchor and, to reassure all those on board in this anxious period of waiting, Duke William ate a large breakfast, which he washed down with spiced wine. Soon the man at the mast-head shouted out that he could see four vessels bearing up on the breeze. Later he announced that the entire Norman fleet was in sight and that it 'made him think of a thick and overgrown forest of trees, all bearing sails'. The coast of England was now clearly visible, and that same morning, 28 September, the invading force landed in Pevensey Bay without meeting any opposition (Tapestry 46–47), thus completing without mishap what has been called 'one of the most important amphibious operations in the history of war'.* King Harold himself was still in York with his army. Such local levies as had been set to guard the southern shore had returned home on 8 September through lack of supplies and because of the pressing need to gather in the harvest. At the same time the English fleet had sailed for London.

William built a rough encampment inside the old Roman fort at Pevensey and left a small garrison there. The next morning, 29 September, he and the

* D. C. Douglas, *William the Conqueror*, p. 195.

main part of his force marched along the coast to Hastings or sailed there in their ships, and there they established a second base (Tapestry 47–53). After a preliminary reconnoitre inland, led by Duke William himself, the Normans spent their time foraging for food, harrying the local inhabitants and ravaging the whole countryside, with the obvious intention of forcing Harold to meet them in battle (Tapestry 48 and 53–54). Meanwhile messengers passed to and fro. Robert, son of Guimara, a Norman resident in England, sent a message to William to tell him of Harold's victory at Stamford Bridge and to warn him of the odds against him (Tapestry 53). An Englishman, who had witnessed the disembarkation in Pevensey Bay, hastened to York to carry the ill tidings to the king.

The news of William's landing is thought to have been brought to Harold in York, although it is possible that when it reached him he had already set out to march back to London with part of his army. Much of his infantry and most of his archers he left behind. Edwin, Earl of Mercia, and Morcar, Earl of Northumbria, refused to accompany him. The men of the shires through which he passed flocked to his banner. He reached London on 6 October, and during the few days which he spent in the city more troops assembled. The monk of Fécamp, whose mission is described by William of Poitiers, arrived with the challenge from the Norman duke, and Harold sent back a message of defiance.

King Harold left London on 12 October or thereabouts, marched with his troops through Kent and Sussex, and late the next day took up a carefully-chosen defensive position on an outlying spur of the South Downs, on the present site of Battle Abbey and the town of Battle. Orderic Vital alone describes the scene of the encounter as 'the spot which used to be called Senlac in ancient times', while the *Anglo-Saxon Chronicle* contents itself with the laconic statement that Harold fought William 'at the hoary apple-tree'. The size of his army is not known. The English writer Florence of Worcester and the Anglo-Norman William of Malmesbury both maintain that Harold's strength was too small for his purpose; but the *Anglo-Saxon Chronicle* says that 'he assembled a large army'. The Norman chroniclers all write of huge numbers. According to William of Poitiers, 'enormous forces of Englishmen had come together from all parts of the country', and the English army 'had a great numerical advantage'. Robert Wace makes Harold boast to Gyrth that he had four hundred thousand men under command, which is quite ridiculous, but elsewhere he admits that many other chroniclers had maintained in retrospect that the English army was too small for the challenge which it faced. The truth is that Harold probably had some seven thousand men and William slightly fewer. Harold massed his men along the brow of the hill, all of them on foot, in dense formation, with himself, his brothers Gyrth and Leofwine, and his picked household troops in the centre. According to William of Poitiers, their weapons were 'javelins and missiles of all sorts', 'axes', and 'stones hafted on wooden handles'. The axes were long-handled and single-bladed. Some of them carried swords. There were very few English archers, only one being portrayed in the Bayeux Tapestry. They stood behind the shield-wall, and those who had protective armour wore helmets and chain-mail hauberks. Their strategy was to hold the line against every attack.

William's camp at Hastings was seven miles from the position chosen by Harold. The arrival of King Harold and his army on 13 October was immediately reported to him. Early the next morning the Normans made their way, some on horseback, some on foot, across the open countryside, until they breasted Telham Down and reached the foot of the hill on which Harold's army was massed (Tapestry 54–60). William of Poitiers imagines the speech (Tapestry 60–64) which the Duke delivered to his men. Henry of Huntingdon, who thinks that the battle was fought 'on Hastings plain', makes this speech even more long-winded and recapitulatory, to the point that in their impatience the Normans actually begin their assault and leave their leader still orating. The Normans themselves held the centre of the invasion army. According to William of Poitiers, they were disposed in three lines: the bowmen stood in front; next came the infantry, armed, some with bows and arrows, others with javelins, but wearing helmets and chain-mail hauberks; the squadrons of cavalry were drawn up behind, with William himself in their midst. The left wing was held by the Poitevins, Bretons and Manceaux, in similar formation, led by Alan Fergant, Count of Brittany. On the right wing fought the men from the Boulonnais and the Ile-de-France, led by Eustace, Count of Boulogne, William FitzOsbern and Roger of Montgomery. The cavalry wore steel helmets with nasals, and chain-mail hauberks; they gripped their reins and their kite-shaped shields in their left fists; in their right hands they held their lances. Their horses had no protective armour (Tapestry 55–56). In the Tapestry, Odo, Bishop of Bayeux, William's half-brother (72), and the duke himself (57 and 60) are armed with clubs or maces; but William of Poitiers makes the duke rally his retreating troops with his lance, and pierce 'shields, helmets, hauberks . . . with savage sword-blows'. As we have seen, the strength of William's army is greatly exaggerated by the chroniclers. In his reply to the message from Robert, son of Guimara, William of Poitiers makes him say: 'If I had only ten thousand men under command of the same temper as the sixty thousand whom I have brought with me, with God to help me and my own brave troops I would still not hesitate to march out to destroy him and his army'. In effect, counting all arms and all ranks, he probably had slightly less than seven thousand men.

The Battle of Hastings lasted throughout the whole of that short Autumn day, Saturday, 14 October 1066 (Tapestry 65–77). The English tactics were to hold the shield-wall along the crest of the hill, and to beat off all assailants by throwing their javelins and by hand-to-hand fighting on foot. William's bow-men shot their arrows at the densely-massed enemy; next the infantry attacked; with their lances, swords and maces the knights then made a frontal assault up the slope. This initial attack was repulsed (Tapestry 69–71), the Norman infantry turned in flight, and many imagined that William had fallen. Holding his mace in his left hand, he pushed back his helmet to show his face to his men (Tapestry 72–73). According to William of Poitiers, he shouted fiercely at his panic-stricken troops and in the end succeeded in turning their rout with his lance. Thousands of the English had broken their shield-wall and pursued the fleeing Normans down the hill. When William and Bishop Odo rallied the Norman army, these were cut off and massacred.

The Normans now made a second concerted attack (Tapestry 73–75). It was led by William himself, Bishop Odo and Robert, son of Roger of Beaumont. After furious fighting it was again repulsed, but in the scrimmage came disaster, for Harold's two brothers, Earl Gyrth and Earl Leofwine, were both killed (Tapestry 67–69). The Normans withdrew once more, this time perhaps as a deliberate tactical manoeuvre, and again the shield-wall broke in exultation and thousands of the English surged forward. While these pursuers were being en-circled and despatched at the foot of the hill, a large force of Norman knights led by William himself managed to gain the crest. King Harold and Duke William both fought with great tenacity and fierce courage. 'Harold hit out repeatedly at every enemy who came within striking distance, dashing horse and horseman to the ground with a single blow, so that none came near him without paying dearly for it,' wrote William of Malmesbury years later. 'It is abundantly clear that it was the duke's bravery which inspired his soldiers as they advanced and gave them courage,' wrote William of Poitiers.

Then came the moment of ultimate disaster for the English defenders. King Harold himself was killed. In the Bayeux Tapestry he is struck down with a sword by a single mounted Norman (76–78). William of Poitiers merely reports the death of Gyrth, Leofwine and Harold as accomplished facts. Guy of Amiens gives a much more complicated and surgical account. '[The duke] called Eustace to his side. He handed over the fighting in that sector to the French and moved up to give all the relief that he possibly could to those who were being slaughtered [by Harold]. Ever keen to do his duty, just as if he, too, had been of the race of Hector, Hugh, the noble heir to Ponthieu, went with them. The fourth man was Giffard, who inherited this name from his father. By the use which they made of their weapons, these four between them encompassed the king's death . . . With the point of his lance the first pierced Harold's shield and then penetrated his chest, drenching the ground with his blood, which poured out in torrents. With his sword the second cut off his head, just below where his helmet protected him. The third disembowelled him with his javelin. The fourth hacked off his leg at the thigh and hurled it far away. Struck down in this way, his dead body lay on the ground.' The story of the arrows shot in the air and of Harold being pierced in the eye is given in the later writers only, William of Malmesbury, Henry of Huntingdon and Robert Wace.

As daylight faded, the English shield-wall broke and those who had the strength to do so turned in flight. In the gathering darkness the Norman knights pursued the fugitives, destroying them mercilessly (Tapestry 79–80). The English made a last desperate stand, in a deep gully on the northern slopes of the battle-field. So fierce was their rally that Eustace, Count of Boulogne, urged William to draw back. As he spoke Eustace was struck a mighty blow between his shoulders, but William continued the carnage with his broken lance.

When all was over, Duke William rode back to the scene of the battle. As best he could in the darkness he surveyed the dead and the dying, and even he was moved to pity – that 'strong and pitiless king', 'brutal, avaricious, and cruel'*. Later the bodies of Gyrth, Leofwine and Harold were with difficulty identified. William refused to surrender the king's mangled corpse to his mother, Gytha, Earl Godwine's widow. At his command it was buried on the sea-shore by William Malet.

* D. C. Douglas, *William the Conqueror*, p. 373 and p. 371.

The year 1066 is the most memorable in our national history. The sequence of events which culminated in Harold's reign of less than ten months is reasonably clear. The problems which the two invasions pose are so numerous that they quite daunt the mind.

For months Harold must have known that William's fleet was lying at anchor first in the estuary of the River Dives and then in the mouth of the River Somme. One or two of Sir Francis Drake's fireships, blown in by the north-westerly breeze which so sorely tried William's patience, would have wrecked the whole enterprise in either river. Such a manoeuvre was inconceivable at the time. Why did the English fleet, which, according to William of Poitiers, was so much on William's mind, not harass the invaders during their crossing? With all their horses on board and all their preparations directed towards a trial of strength on land, the Normans were very vulnerable. In the *Anglo-Saxon Chronicle* the English fleet is said to have left the south coast for London on 8 September, and many ships had been lost in transit. Why was William not driven off when the moment came for him to land in Pevensey Bay? The army set to guard the coast of Sussex had to be disbanded at the same time as the fleet was recalled, for lack of supplies and because the men needed to go home to harvest their crops. Had it not been for his brother Tosti's treachery and treason which resulted directly in the Norwegian invasion, would King Harold have succeeded in beating Duke William and his army? It seems very probable. Was it humanly possible for Harold to march with an army from London to York on 22-25 September, win the savage Battle of Stamford Bridge against King Harold Hardraada on 25 September, march back from York to London with a much depleted army only a few days later, continue his march as far as the Sussex Downs on 12-13 October, and beat the Normans at the Battle of Hastings on 14 October? The account of William of Poitiers shows how very close the English came to victory, and William can hardly be said to have been prejudiced in Harold's favour. However well placed, the English army must have been desperately tired after its long march. William's troops were fresh and they caught their enemy at a grave disadvantage. Why did Harold not wait? He had everything to gain by delaying the encounter. He had only seven thou-sand weary men under command on the morning of 14 October, and he lacked experienced infantry and bowmen. Delay would surely have brought English reinforcements, but every day which passed was an anxiety to the Normans. When Harold drew up his shield-wall on the crest of the Sussex Downs, he must have sent back a great number of horses. Why did he not keep in reserve a support-group of cavalry, hidden on either wing, or on one only, and throw it into the battle at a critical moment? Such a manoeuvre could hardly have failed to be decisive. In his imaginary battle of Saussy between Arthur and Romans, Geoffrey of Monmouth describes such tactics.* Presumably such a move was completely foreign to Harold's concept of fighting; and Geoffrey was writing seventy years later. William made wonderful use of his bowmen at the Battle of Hastings, even if we leave on one side the later story of the arrows shot into the air. In the battle-scenes in the Bayeux Tapestry (65, 75–76) the shields of the Harold's fighting-men are stuck thick with Norman arrows. Why were there no English bowmen? As we have seen, only one is portrayed in the Tapestry, and he is a poor miserable little man without even a quiver (65). A shower of well-directed arrows from the English side would have wiped out the Norman bowmen, and would have wrought havoc among the infantry and the cavalry as they scrambled up the slope. Having fought at William's side in Brittany, Harold must have known the devastating effect of a cavalry attack, however un-coordinated, when covered by a force of archers; but he had left his bowmen behind in the north.

At the Battle of Hastings both sides fought with indescribable bravery. Both leaders showed immense courage and steadfastness. It was the old method of warfare pitted against the new: an army densely massed on foot and on the defensive resisting an army on the attack and on horseback. William clearly had many moments of acute anxiety during that fateful October day, and one can only admire his resource and the way in which he met each contingency as it arose. With his eyes turned anxiously now to the south, then to the north, then to the south again, Harold made such preparations as he could to meet the double invasion of his country. Again we can only admire the masterly control of political, military and maritime logistics which Duke William showed as he made ready for his campaign.

On 25 December 1066 Duke William was crowned King of England in Westminster Abbey by Archbishop Ealdred. Looking back across the centuries and taking a long view, historians see this as a good thing for England: it must have seemed very different to the men and women of the country at the time. Until John lost Normandy in 1203–4, England and the Duchy across the Channel continued to be ruled by William's descendants. When he was elected

* *Historia Regum Britanniæ*, X. 6–12.

to the throne in 1399, Henry IV was the first King of England since Harold whose mother tongue was English.

AUTHOR'S NOTE

I myself have translated anew into modern English all the texts quoted in this book. This includes not only the shorter quotations which support my argument but also the two long passages taken from William of Poitiers. When I have occasion to call the attention of the reader to some specific section of the Bayeux Tapestry, the reference given is to the numbered reproductions at the back of the book.

the authorities

We see the Battle of Hastings and the events which preceded it through the eyes of four Normans born in the Duchy before the invasion and then through those of three Anglo-Normans, if one may use this term for the first generation of mixed parentage fathered on English women by the invaders.

If it is true that the Tapestry was commissioned by Bishop Odo for the consecration of his cathedral in Bayeux in 1077, it is one of the oldest of our sources of information. It is certainly the most detailed. There is no direct evidence, but one presumes that the extremely talented artist who sketched in the outline designs on the linen cloth was a Norman; and, indeed, the most cursory examination of the story depicted on the Tapestry makes the contrary most unlikely. The Tapestry's great importance will be discussed on pp. 60–64 of this book.

About five years after the invasion, and while teams of women were probably engaged in embroidering the Bayeux Tapestry, two authoritative accounts of the events were being composed. The *Gesta Normannorum Ducum* [The History of the Dukes of the Normans], by William of Jumièges, divided into eight books, covers the period from the invasion of Normandy by Hastingus, the legendary forefather of William's line, down to the Battle of Hastings itself, which is described in Book VII, 34–36. In effect, Book VII goes on to include the death of William the Conqueror in 1087, and Book VIII continues the story until the death of Henry I in 1135 and beyond; but this later material was added by Robert de Torigny and Orderic Vital. William of Jumièges is supposed to have written his very succinct account of the events depicted in the Tapestry in the year 1070 or thereabouts. According to him, Earl Harold was sent across the Channel expressly by King Edward the Confessor 'so that he might make a promise of fealty to the duke concerning the king's crown, and confirm this by a series of oaths in the Christian way' (VII. 31). His description of the invasion fills only three short chapters (VII. 34–36), and of the death of the King he says incorrectly: 'Harold himself fell mortally wounded in the very first coming together of the armies' (VII. 36).

Unlike that of William of Jumièges, the narrative of William of Poitiers, *Gesta Guillelmi Ducis Normannorum et Regis Anglorum* [The History of William, Duke of the Normans and King of the English], written *c.* 1073, is long and detailed. A new translation of those chapters which describe the events shown in the Bayeux Tapestry is printed on pp. 33–55 of this book, and to it is prefixed an account of William himself.

A Latin poem of 835 lines, which was rediscovered in 1836 only and to which the title *Carmen de Hastingae proelio* [The Song of the Battle of Hastings] has been given, describes events from the moment in August 1066 when William's fleet lay at anchor in the Dives estuary until his consecration as King of England on 25 December of that same year. This is thought to be the narrative poem ascribed by both Robert de Torigny and Orderic Vital to Guy, uncle of Count Guy of Ponthieu, who was Bishop of Amiens from 1058 until 1075. According to its most recent editors it was written before 11 May 1068. If that statement is true, and it is challenged, the *Carmen* is our earliest source, apart from the *Anglo-Saxon Chronicle*. If it is not true, the *Carmen* is probably an adaptation of the *Gesta* of William of Poitiers. The extremely detailed description which it gives of the death of King Harold is printed above on page 20. This account may well be fictional.

We come now to the three Anglo-Norman writers. The first, William of Malmesbury, is supposed to have been born *c.* 1095, possibly in Wiltshire, Dorset or Somerset. In his *Gesta Regum Anglorum* [The History of the Kings of the English], he tells us that he was of mixed parentage – 'I was born the child of both peoples . . .' (Book III, Prologue) – and he maintains that his account of events is therefore impartial. He is supposed to have finished the first version of the *Gesta* in 1125. The story of the happenings depicted in the Bayeux Tapestry, from Harold's visit to Normandy until his death at the Battle of Hastings, is given in some detail in Book III, §§. 236, 238–245. William describes the battle and concludes: '. . . but when Harold fell dead with his brain pierced by a blow from an arrow, the English fled headlong through the night' (III.242). He devotes a few sad words to a consideration of the results of the battle. 'This was a fateful day for England, a sad destruction of our beloved fatherland, for it now passed into the hands of new masters' (III.245). He discusses the drinking habits of the English and goes on: 'Hence it came about that, when they met William in battle, it was bravado and mad fury which drove them on, rather than any military skill. In this single conflict they doomed them-selves and their homeland to slavery, for they allowed William to win an easy victory' (III.245).

Henry, Archdeacon of Huntingdon, was born *c.* 1080 in the Cambridge-shire and Huntingdonshire fen-country, probably near Ramsey Abbey. He was the son of a priest called Nicholas, who was attached to the Church in Lincoln and who himself, in all probability, had later become Archdeacon of Cam-bridge, Huntingdon and Hertford. Henry was brought up in the household of Robert Bloet, Bishop of Lincoln *c.* 1093–1123. Alexander of Blois, who suc-ceeded Robert as Bishop in 1123, was Henry's patron and encouraged him to write the *Historia Anglorum* [The History of the English], which he began in the late 1120s. It was to Alexander that Geoffrey of Monmouth dedicated *The Prophecies of Merlin* which form Book VII of the *Historia Regum Britanniae* [The History of the Kings of Britain], finished in 1136. Henry accompanied Theo-bald, Archbishop of Canterbury, in whose household Thomas Becket was to serve as a young man and whom he was later to succeed as archbishop, when he went to Rome in 1139 to receive the pallium. On the way he visited the monastery of Bec, where Theobald had once been abbot.

The earliest version of the *Historia Anglorum* runs from the coming of Julius Caesar to Britain until 1129, but Henry later continued it to the death of Stephen in 1154. Writing some sixty years after the events depicted in the Bayeux Tapestry, Henry obviously lacked the first hand information of William of Poitiers, but he made up for this by including a number of fanciful details. On his father's side he was presumably a Norman and his account is a biased one. He describes at some length the oath which Harold is supposed to have sworn to Duke William, thus presenting the English king throughout as a perjuror (6.25). After his account of the death of Gruffydd ap Llywelyn (6.25), he inserts three legendary stories which are much to the discredit of Earl Harold and his brother Tosti: their frenzied quarrel in front of King Edward in Winchester, which is really a tale of boyhood pique taken from the *Vita Beati Edvardi Regis et Confessoris*, lines 358–366 (Luard, p. 372); the murder of a farmer and his family, which seems to be fiction; and the pickling of dead men's legs, heads and arms in casks of wine and beer destined for the king's table, a gruesome deed really done by Caradoc, the son of Gruffydd, according to Florence of Worcester (*Chronicon ex Chronicis, sub anno* 1065), but which Henry ascribes to Tosti. From this point Henry tells the story in its natural sequence: the banishing of

Earl Tosti from Northumbria and his replacement by Earl Morcar (6.26); the death of Edward the Confessor and the election of Harold as King (6.27); Duke William's preparations for the invasion (6.26); Tosti's expedition up the River Humber, his search for help from overseas, the invasion by King Harold Hardraada and the Battle of Stamford Bridge. In his description of this battle he does what he can to detract from Harold Godwineson's glory (6.27). The crossing of the Channel by Duke William and his landing in Pevensey Bay is reported in one sentence (6.28). William of Poitiers had given the duke's speech to his troops before the Battle of Hastings in the third person and with some restraint (*Gesta*, 2.15). Henry makes a long rhetorical exercise of it in direct speech, larding it with historical references which he took from William of Jumièges (*Gesta*, I.5–11; II.12; II.17; IV.17; V.17; VII.26, etc.); and this is a disaster, for not only is it inaccurate in its details (the confusion of Duke Richard II and Robert le Diable; the alleged death of Ralph of Montdidier at the battle of Mortemer), but it ends in bathos, for he makes the impatient Normans begin the attack and leave their duke still speaking (6.30). In his speech Duke William stresses Harold's perjured oath, and makes much play of the murder of the Atheling Alfred thirty years before. His most important statement is the jibe at the English, 'this people which has come here without even a quiverful of arrows' (6.29), for that was to be one of the prime causes of his victory. Even now Henry cannot bring the two armies to grips, for he describes at length the juggling feats of Taillefer, taken from the *Carmen*, 389–408, where he is given the name of Incisor-Ferri, and to be elaborated later by Robert Wace in *Le roman de Rou* and by Geoffroi Gaimar in the *Estorie des Engleis*. In the circumstances, these are ludicrous. Unlike William of Poitiers, Henry had never been a fighting-man: his account of the Battle of Hastings is clear enough, but it is telescoped and not very accurate. He includes the seizure of the Standard, which is given a passing mention in both the *Carmen*, 375, and William of Malmesbury (*Gesta*, III.241), but is not there the object of any special attack. He also has Harold shot in the eye. As a churchman with literary pretensions, he ends his account with the founding of Battle Abbey, – Sanctus Martinus de Bello –, and the curious jingling couplet about Halley's Comet:

> Anno milleno sexageno quoque seno
> Anglorum metae flammas sensere cometae.

Orderic Vital was born near Shrewsbury *c.* 1075, the eldest son of an English woman married to Odelerius, the Norman confessor and adviser of Roger II of Montgomery, 1st Earl of Shrewsbury. Most of his life he spent as a monk in the monastery of Saint Evroult near Lisieux. His *Historia Ecclesiastica* [The History of the Church] was composed in thirteen books between 1123 and 1141. He is not unsympathetic to the English cause. In the *Historia* he records that when, at the age of ten, he first arrived at his monastery in Normandy, he could not understand the language, and he repeatedly calls himself Vitalis Angligena [Vital of English extraction]. Writing nearly seventy years after the events, he maintains that King Edward the Confessor had granted the succession to the English throne to Duke William through the agency of Robert of Jumièges, Archbishop of Canterbury, presumably before that prelate's expulsion in 1052, and that Earl Harold was later sent to Normandy expressly to confirm this, swearing his oath before William and the assembled Norman barons in Rouen and taking part in the expedition against the Bretons after this. He adds a most sympathetic pen-portrait of Harold: 'The Englishman was much admired for his great stature and elegance, for his bodily strength, for his quick-wittedness and verbal facility, his sense of humour and his honest bearing' (III.11). He tells the story of King Edward's death and Harold's election, of the preparations for the invasion and of Tosti's first expedition (III.11). He describes King Harold Hardraada's invasion and the Battle of Stamford Bridge, and then Duke William's invasion and the Battle of Hastings, 'the spot which used to be called Senlac in ancient times' (III.14). According to him, Harold died early in the engagement, before his brother Leofwine: 'Battle was joined in the fiercest fashion from the third hour of the day onwards, and as the two armies made contact King Harold himself was killed' (III.14). His personal touches are the description of Harold, the heaps of English and Norwegian bones still to be seen on the site of the Battle of Stamford Bridge (see p. 15), the name Senlac, and this killing of King Harold so early in the day, which is, however, taken from William of Jumièges. There is no mention of arrows shot into the air.

The master-artist of the Bayeux Tapestry was no doubt a Norman. William of Jumièges, William of Poitiers and Guy of Amiens were assuredly born in Normandy. William of Malmesbury, Henry of Huntingdon and Orderic Vital were the offspring of Norman fathers and English mothers. There remains an eighth Norman authority, Robert Wace, a Jerseyman who studied in Paris and Caen, later becoming 'clerc lisant' in Caen itself, and who between 1160 and 1174 wrote *Le roman de Rou* [The romance of Rollo] in Continental Norman-

French verse for Henry II and his wife Eleanor. He gives the whole story, with many embellishments, some of which he inherited, in Part III, 5456–8972. He makes King Harold a coward, who quarrels with Gyrth before the Battle of Hastings and wants to return to London for reinforcements (7010–7076); as a result he is forced to elaborate Gyrth into a great hero, who exhorts the English army before the battle (7225–7294); he develops the role of Taillefer and makes him intone *La chanson de Roland* to the Norman troops before the engagement (8013–8040); and he describes at great length the arrows shot into the air and the resulting death of Harold: 'The Norman archers took their bows and shot swarms of arrows at their enemies, but the English protected themselves with their shields and none was actually wounded. No matter how carefully they aimed, no matter how skilfully they shot, the Norman bowmen did no damage to the English. They then thought of the idea of shooting up into the air: as their arrows came down they would land on the Englishmen's heads, or hit them full in the face. They carried out this plan and shot their arrows high above their enemies. As the arrows came down, they fell on top of the Englishmen's heads, thudding into their skulls and faces, and even piercing their eyes, so that they were afraid to stick their heads out round their shields and some even kept their eyes shut. The arrows flew through the air thicker than wind-driven rain. The English call them 'billets' and the air was full of them. Then it happened that, as it whistled down out of the sky, one of these arrows struck Harold just above his right eye. In great anguish he dragged it out, snapping it in half and throwing it on the ground; but it had put his eye out. He was in great pain from this wound in his head, and he collapsed forward on his shield. Among the English there is to this day a jingle which they often recite when they are talking to Frenchmen:

> The arrow which struck Harold's eye
> Was straight and strong. Down from the sky
> It screamed, delighting all the French
> Who cheered to see blind Harold blench' (8139–8174).

This may be good writing; but it is not good history. Like Taillefer, who

> 'Devant le duc alout chantant
> De Karlemaigne e de Rollant,
> E d'Oliver e des vassals
> Qui morurent en Rencevals' (8015–8018),

we have strayed into the realm of literature.

The only eleventh-century English accounts of the Battle of Hastings and the events which preceded it are those contained in the *Anglo-Saxon Chronicle*. As is well known, the *Chronicle* exists in six manuscripts, which differ considerably from each other and only three of which have anything to offer which is relevant to our purpose; MS. C, copied in Abingdon, British Museum, Cotton, Tiberius B. i; MS. D, possibly copied in York, British Museum, Cotton, Tiberius B. iv; and MS. E, possibly copied in Peterborough, Bodleian Library, Laud, Misc. 636. None mentions Harold's visit to Normandy in 1063 or 1064. All describe the expulsion of Earl Tosti, his return with a hostile fleet and the later events which led up to the Battle of Stamford Bridge. C then stops. D gives the following brief description of the Battle of Hastings: 'The news was brought to King Harold, and he assembled a large army and marched to meet William at the hoary apple-tree. William attacked him before his troops were drawn up in formation. King Harold and all those who supported him resisted William strongly, and there were heavy casualties on both sides. King Harold was killed in the battle, and so were his brother Earl Leofwine, and Earl Gyrth, his other brother, together with many brave men. The French remained masters of the field. God granted them this victory because of the people's sins.' E is even more succinct: 'Harold marched from the north and met William in battle before all his army had arrived. He was killed there, and his two brothers Gyrth and Leofwine with him.'

There remains the twelfth-century *Chronicon ex Chronicis* [The Chronicle taken from other Chronicles], the earliest version of which tells the story of the English people from the landing of Hengist and Horsa in 450 until the year 1117, soon after which, according to one of his continuers, the original author died. As we have seen on p. 11, the monk Florence of Worcester, if, indeed, he was the author of this part of the work, gives an admiring account of all that Harold did during his short reign. Florence seems to have been an Englishman and, apart from the *Anglo-Saxon Chronicle*, to which he owes a considerable debt, his *Chronicon* is the only prime source to give an English point of view. He does not mention the oath of 1063 or 1064, or, indeed, Harold's visit to Normandy. He praises Harold for the bravery which he showed both at Stamford Bridge and Hastings, and he laments his death, of which he gives no details: 'Many met their death on this side and that, and then, alas, just as twilight was falling, the king himself was killed' (*Chronicon, sub anno* 1066). Florence considers that Harold fought the second battle too soon after the first and with insufficient troops. On the first point, at least, Harold would no doubt have agreed with him. It is Florence who, before he was elected king, calls Harold Godwineson 'subregulus', to make the point that he was Edward's deputy and natural successor.

william of poitiers

William of Poitiers was a Norman, born in Préaux (Eure). His sister became Abbess of the nunnery of Saint-Léger de Préaux. In his youth he had been a fighting-man. He was sent to study in Poitiers *c.* 1047–1048, or a little before. He took orders and became chaplain to Duke William, whom he accompanied on certain of his military expeditions in Anjou, Maine and Brittany (1053–1064). He was made Archdeacon of Lisieux by Bishop Hugh, who occupied the see from 1050 to 1077. He was not present at the Battle of Hastings, but he crossed to England some time after the invasion. He outlived Duke William, become King of England, who died in 1087.

William of Poitiers' book, *Gesta Guillelmi Ducis Normannorum et Regis Anglorum* [The History of William, Duke of the Normans and King of the English], exists only in a version copied providentially by André du Chesne from a manuscript, now lost, which then belonged to Sir Robert Cotton. This copy was published by André du Chesne in 1619 (*Historiae Normannorum scriptores antiqui*, pp. 178–213). Both the beginning and the end are missing. As we have it, the story runs from the death of Canute in 1035 to the assassination of Copsi, Earl of Northumbria, in 1067. William of Poitiers seems to have written his *Gesta c.* 1073–1074. According to the most recent editor, Raymonde Foreville, his essential source was his personal experience as a young fighting-man and then as chaplain to Duke William, and the information which he would have received orally during his close acquaintance with William, become king, and with the knights and churchmen of his court. His secondary sources were, possibly, the Bayeux Tapestry itself, and, probably, Book VII of the *Gesta Normannorum Ducum* [The History of the Dukes of the Normans] by William of Jumièges. If the *Carmen de Hastingae proelio* [The Song of the Battle of Hastings] really was written before 1068, he may well have used that; on the other hand, Guy of Amiens, who lived on until 1075, always provided that it was he who wrote the *Carmen*, may well have copied William. It is a tangled skein. William's account of the Battle of Hastings and the happenings which led up to it is, naturally enough, strongly biased in Duke William's favour, and it is larded with references to and imitations from the classics, notably Caesar, Virgil, Sallust, Cicero, Statius, Juvenal, Tacitus and Suetonius.

The *Gesta* is by far the most complete account written in the eleventh century which we have of the happenings depicted in the Tapestry. What follows is a new translation of chapters 1.41 to 1.46 and 2.1 to 2.25.

Edward, King of the English, loved William [of Normandy] as much as if the duke had been his brother or his son, and he had long before appointed him as his heir. It was at this time that Edward gave William a pledge even more binding than any which he had proffered so far. By the very sanctity of his way of life he was a man constantly preoccupied with the next world. He now felt that his own hour was fast approaching, and he therefore determined to make all possible preparations for his death. In order to confirm his promise by an oath, he sent Harold to William, Harold, the wealthiest of all his subjects, the most powerful and the most highly honoured. Some time before, Harold's brother [Wulfnoth] and his nephew [Hakon] had been handed over to William as hostages, in an attempt to secure this same succession. In sending Harold, King Edward behaved with the utmost wisdom, for, with his wealth and his authority, Harold was the man to contain any revolt of the English, if, with that perfidy and restlessness which they so often display, they were to rise in revolt.

On his way to carry out the business entrusted to him, Harold experienced some danger during the crossing. He landed on the coast of Ponthieu, but there he fell into the hands of Count Guy. He and his party were seized and thrown into prison. I have no doubt that so great a nobleman would have preferred shipwreck to such ignominy. Their lust for gain has led certain local groups of French people to adopt an execrable custom, which is quite barbarous and devoid of any touch of Christian justice. They seize the persons of men who are in high place or who are very wealthy. They throw them into prison, heap insults upon them and even torture them. When their victims are almost at death's door as the result of the miseries which they have endured, they let them go, but only in exchange for an enormous ransom.

When Duke William discovered what had happened to the envoys who were on their way to him, he sent his own messengers with orders that they should free Harold by simple request or, if necessary, by threats. Count Guy behaved very well. He could have tortured Harold, and either cut his throat or ransomed him, just as the fancy took him; but he resisted these temptations and rode with him to Eu castle, where he handed him over to William. Guy was rewarded amply enough, for William conveyed to him several vast and valuable estates, adding a considerable sum of money into the bargain. William received Harold with great honour, taking him off to the city of Rouen, which was the capital of the Duchy. There he treated Harold and his party most hospitably, for he wanted to cheer them up and make them forget the hazards of their journey. William had every reason to congratulate himself on this important guest, who had come to him as the envoy of his close relation and dearest friend. He naturally hoped that Harold would mediate faithfully between himself and the English people, who held him second only to their king.

A council was convened at Bonneville-sur-Touques and there, according to the sacred rite of Christian people, Harold swore an oath of fidelity to William. A number of extremely famous men who are not given to lying, whose word can be trusted and who, moreover, were present and witnessed the event, have told how, freely and distinctly, as the last article of his oath, Harold made the following deposition: that he would act as William's representative at the court of his master, King Edward, as long as that king remained alive; that after Edward's death he would do everything in his power, by exercising his authority and by using his vast wealth, to confirm William in his succession to the throne of England; that in the meantime he would entrust to the duke's military representatives Dover castle, to the fortification of which he would give his own personal attention, paying for it with his own funds; and finally that he would hand over other castles in such districts of that country as the duke might wish to fortify, and that he would provide the garrisons with all the food they needed. The duke took Harold's two hands in his and received his homage. Then, just before Harold made his oath, the duke received his petition, and confirmed him in the possession of his lands and all his functions. Edward was already ill and he was not expected to live long.

William knew that Harold was keen on fighting and only too ready to add to his laurels, so he fitted him and his party out with the weapons of war, provided them with mettlesome horses, and led them off to take part in the war in Brittany. Harold was William's guest and he had come as an envoy: now the duke made him his comrade-in-arms, in the hope that, by doing him this honour, he might ensure that he remained faithful and obedient. In its overweening arrogance the whole of Brittany had risen in arms against Normandy.

Conan, the son of Alan, was the leader in this rash enterprise. As he grew to man's estate, he became more and more arrogant. For a long time he had been under the guardianship of his uncle Eudo, but he freed himself, wrapped Eudo in chains and threw him into prison. Then with great truculence he started to rule over the province which he had inherited from his father. He stirred up again the revolt which his father had once led, for he had made up his mind to be the enemy of Normandy and not its vassal. By ancient right William was not only ruler of the Normans but Conan's overlord as well. William ordered a castle called Saint James to be constructed on the frontier where Normandy faces Brittany, for he was determined to prevent starving pillagers from crossing over to rob and ravage the unprotected churches and the far-flung village communities of these borderlands. It was Charles [the Simple], King of the Franks, who bought peace and the alliance of Rollo, the first Duke of the Normans and the progenitor of all the other dukes who were to come after him. Charles gave his daughter Gisela to Rollo in marriage and handed Brittany over to him for the Normans to rule for ever. The Franks actually asked for this Treaty [of Saint-Clair-sur-Epte], for, even with the sword of the Gauls to assist them, they could no longer resist the Danish axe. There is plenty of evidence for this in the pages of our Annals. On a number of occasions the Counts of Brittany strove their hardest to shake off the yoke of Norman domination, but they never succeeded. Alan and Conan were close blood-relations of the Dukes of Normandy, and as a result they resisted those dukes with even greater courage. In the end Conan became so arrogant that he had the nerve to announce the actual day on which he proposed to cross the frontiers of Normandy. By nature he was a very savage man, and he was at the height of his physical strength. His lands stretched far and wide, his men were devoted to him, and Brittany produced an incredible number of warriors.

In those parts each fighting-man fathers another fifty, for, according to their barbarous ways of going on, he is apportioned ten or more women. They say that the same was true of the Moors in ancient times, for they knew nothing of God's law or of personal restraint. The immense hordes of people which result show little interest in cultivating the fields or developing the arts of civilization, for they spend all their time rushing about on horseback and practising with their weapons. They drink a lot of milk, but they do not have much bread to eat. Their extensive meadow-lands, which hardly know what harvest means, offer rich pasture to their flocks. When they are not actually at war they occupy their time in robbery, brigandage and family feuds, to keep their hands in, as it were. In battle they engage the enemy with savage alacrity: and when they are actually fighting they rage like lunatics. They are used to driving all before them, but they themselves rarely give in. They rejoice in victory and in honour won on the battlefield, and on these subjects they are given to endless boasting. They take great pleasure in quarrelling over the booty which they have stripped from the dead: with them this is an honourable pastime and one which they enjoy immensely.

Duke William cared not a straw for all this horror. On the very day which, as he well recalled, Conan had appointed for his own advance, he himself invaded Brittany. Like a man who sees the lightning-flash come perilously near, Conan fled at full speed to the positions which he had prepared, abandoning the siege of Dol, which was one of his own castles. Dol played no part in the rebel uprising, for it remained faithful to the just cause. Rivoallon, the lord of the castle, tried to hold Conan. Sarcastically he called him back, begging him to wait for forty-eight hours, for that would be enough for him to pay his ransom. The poor man was terrified: he continued his retreat and would not stay his course; everything he heard made him more frightened still. Meanwhile the awesome battle-leader who pursued him would have pressed on behind him in his flight had he not perceived the obvious danger of leading so large an army through this open countryside, where there were no supplies and no known roads. In this barren land, if anything at all remained from the previous year's harvest, the local inhabitants had hidden it away in safe retreats, together with their flocks. The corn was green and still stood in the ear. William therefore turned his army back, harassed as it was by this lack of provisions. He was afraid that his troops might be encouraged to plunder church lands, if they came to any, and, in his magnanimous way, he imagined that Conan would soon beg grace and pardon for the crime which he had committed. William had no sooner withdrawn from Breton territory than it was reported to him unexpectedly that Geoffrey of Anjou had joined Conan with an immense force, and that both leaders were preparing to attack him the very next day. The prospect of battle filled Duke William with delight, for he realized that it would be all the more glorious to triumph in a single fight over two separate enemies, each of them so formidable. What is more, the advantages of such a victory would be immense.

However, Rivoallon, in whose territory they pitched their tents, was loud in his complaints. He would have been grateful to William, he said, for rescuing him from his enemy, if the damage which he was doing had not cancelled out all the gain. If William were to make his stand there to meet the enemy army, this tract of land, which was not very fertile anyway, and which had already been sadly ravaged, would be completely ruined. What difference would it make to the local peasantry if they lost the labour of a whole year through a Norman army instead of through a Breton one? The expulsion of Conan had brought Rivoallon some measure of fame, but it had done nothing to preserve his property. The duke replied that Rivoallon must realize that any hasty withdrawal would be a disgrace. He promised full payment in ready money for any damage which might be done. He forbade his troops to do any harm to Rivoallon's crops or his cattle. They obeyed this order with such scrupulous care that a single stook of corn would have sufficed as recompense for all the harm which they did. They waited in vain for the enemy onslaught; but Conan continued his retreat.

Duke William returned to his base. He kept Harold with him as his guest for some time. Then he loaded him with presents and sent him on his way. By doing this he paid his respects both to King Edward, at whose order Harold had come, and to Harold himself, who had undertaken the mission. What is more, one of the two hostages, Harold's nephew [Hakon], went back with him, for to please his guest Duke William gave him his liberty.

These, then, are the reproaches made against you, Harold. After all these kindnesses, how could you dare to deprive Duke William of his inheritance and to make war on him, you who, by an oath so sacrosanct, had bound yourself and all your people to him, placing your hands in his and swearing fealty? It was for you to hold the Englishmen in check. Instead you most perniciously encouraged them in their revolt. The following winds which swelled your coalblack sails as you journeyed homewards brought nothing but unhappiness. You horrid man! The calm sea-waters which permitted you to cross back to your native shore must ever be accursed. The quiet harbour where you landed must bear its brunt of shame, for with you came the most disastrous shipwreck ever suffered by your fatherland . . .

The news was received quite unexpectedly of an event which turned out to be true: England had lost King Edward and Harold had been crowned in his place. This headstrong Englishman had not waited for the result of a public election. With the backing of a number of blackguardly partisans, he had broken his plighted word and occupied the royal throne by popular acclama⁄tion, on the very day when, in the midst of mourning and with all his people plunged in grief, the good king was being laid to rest. Harold was crowned by Stigand, in a ceremony which was not acceptable to God, for the archbishop had been deposed from his priestly ministry and excommunicated by the pope in his wisdom and zeal.

Duke William sought the advice of his supporters, and then decided to avenge this insult and lay claim to his inheritance by force of arms. It is true that quite a few of his leaders did their utmost to dissuade him from it, as an enterprise at once too difficult and far beyond the natural resources of Normandy. In addition to its bishops and abbots, Normandy had among its advisers at that time a number of outstanding laymen, who added great distinction and renown to its council⁄meetings: Robert, Count of Mortain; Robert, Count of Eu, the brother of Hugh, Bishop of Lisieux, whose activities I have described in a previous chapter; Richard, Count of Evreux, the son of Archbishop Robert; Roger of Beaumont; Roger of Montgomery; William FitzOsbern: and Hugh the Viscount. Thanks to the wisdom and energy of these men, she had no occasion to fear for her safety. With such men to help her, the Republic of Rome would have had no need for two hundred senators, even supposing that in our days it had still retained its erstwhile power. What is more, in all their deliberations, as I myself know full well, these men recognized the wisdom of their lawful prince, as if, by some divine inspiration, he knew in advance what was best to be done and what was better left undone. 'To those who act accord⁄ing to His dictates, God gives wisdom', as someone has said who knew His will. From his childhood onwards Duke William has been God⁄fearing in all his behaviour. When he has given an order no⁄one has disobeyed it, unless there were some cogent reason for doing so.

It would be too tedious to describe in full detail how, in his great wisdom, the duke had ships constructed and how he fitted them out with weapons, crews, supplies of food and all that is necessary for the conduct of war. Everyone in Normandy applied himself energetically to the task. With equal foresight William nominated those who were to rule over Normandy and protect its frontiers during his absence. A strong force of fighting-men came to join him from foreign parts, attracted no doubt by his well-known generosity, but all trusting in the justice of his cause. He forbade all looting. At his own expense he had fifty thousand troops to feed, and this for a whole month while contrary winds held them back in the mouth of the River Dives. He was wise and moderate in all his decisions: to make sure that no-one stole or looted, ample supplies were distributed to the knights who had come to join him. The peasants' herds and flocks grazed peacefully in the fields and heathlands. In all security the harvest waited for the husbandman's sickle, with no proud rout of horsemen to tread it down and no forager to steal it. With no-one to protect him and no weapon in his hand, the countryman turned his horse's head wherever he willed, singing as he went: even if he saw a squadron of knights approaching, he had no reason for fear.

At this time Saint Peter's throne was occupied by Pope Alexander, a man worthy to be obeyed by all. The universal Church listened to his pronounce-ments, and the decisions which he made were always just and salutary. Before this he was Bishop of Lucca. He had no desire whatsoever for promotion, yet he was raised to the highest place of all by the violent lobbying of a group of people who were then all-powerful in Rome. He was given a massive majority by the College of Cardinals, and so became master and mentor of the bishops of the entire world. By the sanctity of his life and the force of his faith he was well worthy of the appointment, and his fame shone bright from East to West. Just as the sun, so changeless in its nature, holds firmly to the confines of its course, so in his own behaviour Pope Alexander observed the strict letter of the truth. He made compromise with no man and, round the wide world, wherever his power reached, he waged war on sin.

Duke William told the pope what he was planning to do and asked for his support. As a symbol of his approval and as a mandate from Saint Peter the pope sent him a banner, behind which he could march in all confidence against the foe. He had recently made a treaty with Henry, the Emperor of the Romans, son of the Emperor Henry and grandson of Conrad, by which it was agreed that Germany would come to his assistance against any enemy, if he called for help. Sweyn, King of Denmark, sent envoys and promised support; but he remained faithful to his alliance with William's enemies, as you will see if you read in the following pages the disasters which befell him.

For his part Harold was only too ready to offer battle on land or sea. He drew up a huge army on the sea-coast, and with great cunning he sent out spies whom he had trained. One of these was captured. As he had been instructed to do he tried to explain his presence by telling lies. In the reply which he gave him Duke William showed his great magnanimity. 'Harold has no need to buy your devotion and industry with his gold and silver,' he said, 'or that of those who have come with you to spy on our activities. My own presence here must surely reveal to him, more plainly than he can wish and, indeed, more quickly than you can, the exact nature of our plans and the purpose of our preparations. Take this message back to him from me. He has nothing adverse to fear from us and he can go on living in peace and security for the rest of his days, provided only that, within the space of one year, he does not see me set foot in the land where he finds sanctuary.'

Many of the Norman leaders were greatly upset by this outspoken defiance, and they made no secret of their anxiety. They magnified the forces which Harold had under command and made little of their own, their lack of faith being only too obvious in what they said. They gave it out that Harold's financial backing was very great, and that with it he would be able to win over to his side many powerful kings and chieftains; he had a vast fleet, manned by sailors most experienced in maritime affairs, inured to the perils of the sea and trained in marine warfare; and in its resources and in the strength of its armed forces his country was infinitely more powerful than ours. What hope was there that the ship-building programme could be completed in the space of one year, or, even if it were, that oarsmen could be found? Who was there who deep in his heart did not fear that by this hastily-planned expedition our most lovely homeland would be reduced to utter misery? Who could deny that even the resources of a Roman Emperor would have been insufficient for such a difficult enterprise?

The duke restored their courage by making the following speech. 'We all know about Harold's military skill,' he said. 'If it fills us with fear, it also raises our expectations. He is using his wealth to no purpose. He may spend his money, but he is powerless to bolster up his throne. He lacks the daring and the strength of purpose to offer even the smallest portion of what those of my faction are prepared to promise. Those possessions, which are really mine, but which he pretends to be his, I hereby offer to you, and they will be distributed as I think fit. The man who is in a position to give away not only his own property but also the land which the enemy actually occupies cannot fail to win the day. We shall not be short of shipping, for we shall soon have a sufficiently large fleet at our disposal. Let our enemies know this for sure, and we ourselves will soon see it come about, if we have any luck at all. Wars are won by courage, not by mere force of numbers. What is more, Harold will be fighting to retain what he has stolen. We, on the other hand, will be striving to gain what we have accepted as a gift, what we have bought by services rendered. This firm conviction of the strength of our cause must set aside all sense of danger: it will ensure our happy triumph, proclaim our honour to the world and make memorable our name.'

This steadfast and far-seeing Christian leader had no doubt at all that Almighty God, who rights all wrongs, would not permit his cause to fail, for it was just. He was the more convinced of this when he recalled that his purpose was not to foster his own fame and fortune, but to set right once more the practice of the Christian religion in those foreign parts.

Soon the whole fleet, so providentially equipped, sailed out from its anchorage in the River Dives and the neighbouring ports, where it had long awaited the southern wind necessary for the crossing, and with a following westerly breeze took up its station off Saint-Valery-sur-Somme. There in all confidence, by his prayers, his donations to the Church and his vows, our duke committed himself to the protection of Almighty God, in no way dismayed by the long delay caused by the contrary wind, or by fear of shipwreck, or even by the cowardly desertion of a great number of knights who had promised their support. Deliberately meeting failure face to face, he kept secret as best he could the death of those who had been drowned, and buried them when no-one was looking. By increasing the daily issue of rations, he made sure that there was no scarcity. He dismissed those who had no stomach for the fight and he encouraged the waverers. In his prayers he called upon God to help him, and he went so far as to have the earthly remains of Saint Valerius, whom God loved, carried in procession from his church, in an attempt to gain a following wind in place of a contrary one. In this display of humility there processed with him the whole force of those who were about to set out to sea.

At length the long-awaited wind began to blow. They raised their voices and their hands to heaven in thanksgiving, encouraging each other with mighty

shouts. Without losing a moment they put out from land and with great enthusiasm began the hazardous crossing. They were determined to set sail without
delay. They rushed on board, their only fear being that they might be left
behind: so that, when one of them shouted to a man-at-arms and another hailed
his boon companion, none had a thought to spare for his own troops, his friends
or even his essential equipment. Meanwhile the duke, hot with excitement,
bellowed orders to anyone whom he saw lagging behind and exhorted them
all to embark.

There was some fear that they might reach the shore towards which they were
sailing just before light and thus run the risk of an unknown and dangerous
anchorage. Through his herald the duke gave an order that, once they were well
out to sea, for some part of the night all the ships should remain at anchor near
to his own vessel. Only when they saw a lantern shining from the top of his
mast would they hear the trumpet sound the signal to advance.

Ancient Greece tells us the tale of how Agamemnon, the grandson of Atreus,
put to sea with a thousand ships to avenge the rape of Helen. I can assure you
that, when he set out to win a royal crown, William had even more. Xerxes is
said to have linked by a bridge of boats the towns of Sestos and Abydos, between
which rolled the sea. I tell you the truth when I say that William united under
one rule the broad lands of Normandy and England. No-one has ever surpassed
William: he has adorned his fatherland with never-to-be-forgotten trophies and
given to it its most signal triumphs. He is the equal of Xerxes, who lost his fleet
and was beaten by a more powerful enemy; and in my opinion he is braver than
Xerxes, anyway.

After riding at anchor for some time the ships set sail again in the darkness.
The vessel carrying the duke pressed on so quickly that it left the others behind,
rushing forward under full sail to victory, as if it wanted to match William's
imperiousness by its own speed. In the morning one of the sailors was ordered to
look out from the masthead to see if the other ships were following after, but he
reported that he could see nothing on the horizon except sea and sky. Anchor was
dropped, and, to prevent his comrades from becoming prey to fear and melan-
choly, our intrepid duke ate a large breakfast and washed it down with spiced
wine, just as if he were in his own dining-hall. He was remarkably gay and
swore that, with God to help them, to whose care he had committed them, the
others would very soon arrive. Virgil himself, whose songs in praise of the
Trojan Aeneas, the founding-father and glory of ancient Rome, have made him

the prince of poets, would not have scorned to describe the sang-froid and strength of purpose which William showed at this meal. When questioned a second time, the watchman said that he could make out four ships which were approaching. On being asked yet again, he shouted down that he could see so many ships that they made him think of a thick and overgrown forest of trees, all bearing sails. The duke's hopes then changed to rejoicing. Just how much he thanked God from the bottom of his heart for His loving-kindness I leave you to imagine.

The wind, which was still in his favour, blew William to Pevensey and there he disembarked without difficulty and without finding any hostile force to resist him. Harold had withdrawn to the region round York, where he was soon to fight a battle against his own brother Tosti and Harold, King of Norway. It was not to be wondered at that this blood-brother, infuriated by the insults which he had received and determined to recover the estates which had been taken from him, was prepared to summon an army from overseas to attack Harold. Although she was not able to bear arms against him, his sister, who, like Tosti, was completely different from Harold in her personal behaviour, opposed him in her every wish and in every plan which she made, for she considered him to be a truculent murderer, a man soiled by loose-living, tireless in his pursuit of other folk's possessions, the sworn foe of equity and fair dealing. This admirable woman, who was intellectually the equal of any man, wanted only to see justice done, the cause of which she furthered all her life. In short she wanted William to rule over the English nation, William whom King Edward her husband had adopted as his son and appointed as his successor, William the wise, the just, the strong.

The Normans landed jubilantly. They built a first fortification at Pevensey and a second one at Hastings, as rallying-points for themselves and as shelters for their ships. Marius and Pompey the Great were both famous men, and each earned a triumph by his cunning and his energy, the former when he brought Jugurtha back to Rome in chains, the latter when he forced Mithridates to poison himself: yet, when they found themselves in enemy territory at the head of a huge army, they did not dare to run the risk of moving forward with a force of legionaries in advance of their line of battle. It was their habit, and it still remains the habit of military commanders, to send reconnaissance troops forward, rather than to go themselves, for they have more concern for their own lives than for the safety of their soldiery. William, on the contrary, rode quickly out with a band of twenty-five knights, no more, to reconnoitre the neighbourhood and question the local inhabitants. Because of the steep incline of the trackway he came back on foot, a circumstance which amused him immensely, and may well amuse my readers. He gained great credit from the fact that he carried on his shoulder, on top of his own chain-mail hauberk, the cuirass of one of his companions, William FitzOsbern, whom he had relieved of this deadweight of metal, although FitzOsbern was renowned for his physical strength and his courage.

A certain wealthy inhabitant of these parts, Norman in origin and Robert by name, the son of a noblewoman called Guimara, sent a messenger to Hastings, to the Duke, his overlord and blood-relation. 'King Harold', went the message, 'has just fought a battle against his own brother and the King of Norway, who was held to be the most powerful man alive. He has killed them both in a single engagement and has wiped out their huge armies. Encouraged by his success, he is now advancing against you by forced marches, at the head of an immensely powerful band of soldiers. In my opinion, compared with his troops, your men are no more than a rabble of miserable curs. You are said to be a prudent man, both in time of peace and time of war, and until now you are thought to have ordered your affairs in a sensible way. Think what you are doing and weigh carefully what you are undertaking, instead of rashly venturing yourself in a battle from which you cannot escape alive. My advice to you is that you should stay inside your fortifications and not engage the enemy in hand-to-hand combat for the moment.' The duke sent the following answer: 'Thank your master for the cautionary message which he has thought fit to send to me, although, indeed, he might have warned me without being so insulting about it. Then tell him this. I shall not take refuge behind protecting walls or earthwork. I shall engage Harold at the first possible opportunity. If I had only ten thousand men under command of the same temper as the sixty thousand whom I have brought with me, with God to help me and my own brave troops I would still not hesitate to march out to destroy him and his army.'

One day when the duke was inspecting the guard set over the ships, just as he was moving from one vessel to another, a message reached him that a monk had arrived as envoy from Harold. He immediately went to see the man, cunningly introducing himself in the following way: 'I am the seneschal of William, Count of the Normans, and his closest confidant. Only through me can you pass your message to him. Tell me what news you bring. The duke will without question accept what I report, for he holds no-one dearer than me. Later on, at a convenient moment, as you yourself choose, you can with my help appear before him and speak.' Once he had heard the monk explain what his message was, the duke ordered this envoy to be received hospitably and to be treated with all due courtesy. In the meantime he considered what reply he should give to the message and took counsel with his advisers.

The next day, seated in the midst of his army commanders, the duke summoned the monk to his presence and said: 'I am William, by the grace of God Prince of the Normans. Now, in the presence of these men, repeat what you told me yesterday'. The envoy made the following answer: 'Harold sends this message to you. You have invaded his country, whether trusting in your own strength or as an act of sheer temerity he cannot tell. He is mindful of the fact that King Edward once nominated you as heir to the kingship of England and that he himself in Normandy confirmed you in this succession. At the same time he is convinced that it is to himself that the kingdom rightly belongs, for his lord the king granted it to him as he lay dying. Since the time when Saint Augustine first came to this land, it has been the common custom of our nation that a testamentary donation made on one's deathbed should be considered as binding. He is therefore within his rights in asking you and your men to leave this country. If you refuse, he will hold as null and void his treaty of friendship with you and all the agreements which he made with you in Normandy, placing the full responsibility upon your head.'

When he had listened to Harold's message, the duke asked the monk if he were willing to conduct an envoy of his own to Harold in all safety. The monk promised that he would take the same care of the envoy's wellbeing as he proposed to take of his own. Thereupon the duke summoned a monk of Fécamp and gave him this message, which he was to carry to Harold without delay. 'I have come to this country in no rash spirit and certainly not wrongfully, but after due consideration and in pursuit of my rights. As Harold himself admits, King Edward, my lord and blood-relation, made me heir to his throne, as recompense for the great honours and numerous benefits which my ancestors and I had afforded to him, his brother and their men, and because, of all the members of his family, he considered me the most worthy and the most able to give him support during his lifetime and to govern his kingdom after his death. He assuredly did not do this without the consent of his leading advisers and the approval of Archbishop Stigand, Count Godwine, Count Leofric and Count Siward. They have confirmed on oath and over their own signatures that after Edward's death they would accept me as their overlord, and that, as long as he lived, they would make no move to take over the country by setting up obstacles against me. The king gave me Godwine's son and grandson as hostages. What is more, he sent Harold himself to Normandy, so that he might swear in person in my presence what his father and the others whom I have men‑ tioned had sworn when I was not there. While he was on his way to me, he was in great danger of being captured, but, thanks to my foresight and courage, he was rescued. He did homage to me with his hands within mine, and he confirmed in writing that the kingship of England should without ques‑ tion be mine. I am prepared to present the case against him in a court of justice, in accordance with the laws of the Normans, or with those of the English, just as he chooses. If in all truth and equity the Normans, or the English, should decree that the kingdom should legitimately be his, let him hold it in peace. If they decide that the legal position is that it should be handed over to me, then he must surrender it to me. If Harold refuses to accept this proposition, I think it wrong that my men and his should lose their lives in battle, seeing that they have no responsibility for our quarrel. I am prepared to hazard my own life against his to prove that the throne of England belongs legally to me and not to him.'

It is my wish that this carefully copied transcript of Duke William's precise words should be made available for all to read, rather than some paraphrase of my own, for in this way I can make sure that he will gain the praise and approval of all. From what I have set before you, it will be clear what a wise, just, pious and courageous man he was. The force of his argument, if you study it carefully – and not even Cicero, the greatest advocate of ancient Rome, could find flaws in it – destroyed the counter‑argument of Harold. He was, in short, prepared to accept the judgement of the nations concerned. Even if they were his enemies, he did not want the English to die as a result of his quarrel. His wish was that the case should be decided in single combat, with his own life at stake.

When the monk reported William's answer to Harold, who was by then not far away, he went pale with terror and remained silent for a long time, as if he had lost the power of speech. The envoy asked him several times what his answer was. First he said: 'Our advance continues'. Then he changed this to: 'We march to victory'. The envoy pressed him to give a fuller answer, making it clear that the Norman duke wanted single combat, not a wholesale slaughter of the two armies. This brave and energetic man preferred to surrender what was just and in his favour, rather than be responsible for the death of a great number of people. He was quite convinced that it was Harold who would be killed, for he was the less brave man and his cause was not a just one. Then Harold raised his face to heaven and exclaimed: 'Let God decide today where justice lies between William and me!' He was so blinded by his lust for the kingship and, in his rash temerity, so oblivious of the wrong which he was doing that, to his ruination, he accepted his own conscience as the true arbiter of his fate.

Meanwhile the experienced knights sent out as scouts at the duke's order reported that the enemy was approaching, for, when he heard that the territory round the Norman encampment was being ravaged, Harold was so furious that he hastened his march. His plan was to make a sudden night attack and to crush his enemies when they were least expecting him. To block their escape he had brought up an armed fleet of seven hundred ships and stationed it out to sea. Without losing a moment, the duke ordered all those in camp to arm themselves, although that day a large section of his troops had gone off foraging. He himself with great devotion took part in the ceremony of the Mass, fortifying his mind and body by taking communion in both kinds. In great humility he suspended round his neck those relics the support of which Harold had sacrificed when, after swearing his oath upon them, he broke his word. There were present two bishops who had come with him from Normandy, Odo of Bayeux and Geoffrey of Coutances, together with a few monks and a great number of priests. By their prayers this band of clergy prepared the way for battle. As William was putting it on, his chain-mail hauberk slipped over to the left and this would have terrified a lesser mortal. He laughed to see it slide, judging it pure chance and not a bad augury sent to frighten him.

I have no doubt that the speech, short in view of the circumstances, with which William roused to fever-heat the courage of his troops, was an extremely fine one, but it has not come down to us in all its eloquent detail. He reminded the

Normans that, under his leadership, they had always been victorious, in the face of great and manifold dangers. He reminded them of their fatherland, of their glorious history, of their immense reputation. The time had come, he said, when they must prove in hand-to-hand combat just how brave they really were and how great was their courage. It was not merely a question of who should survive to rule, but of who should escape with his life from this immense peril. If they fought like men, theirs would be the victory, the honour, the material gain. If not, they would be slaughtered like cowards, or, if taken prisoner, they would earn for themselves the disgrace of eternal ignominy. There was no way open for retreat: in front they were blocked by an army and by an unknown countryside which was hostile to them; behind them lay the sea and the promise of more fighting. Men should not be frightened by mere force of numbers. Time and time again the English had been conquered by force of arms and had fallen in battle; they had repeatedly been beaten by their opponents and had surrendered to them; they had no reputation whatsoever for prowess on the battlefield. Lack-ing experience of military affairs, they would easily be overcome by a small force of brave and determined men, the more so as assistance from on high could not fail the Normans in their just cause. They must be daring, they must never yield and in less than no time they would rejoice in victory.

The Normans moved forward as follows in a well-ordered line of battle, march-ing behind the standard which the pope had given to them. In the first line William placed his infantry, armed with bows and arrows. In the second line he placed more infantry, better armed and wearing hauberks. Behind them came the squadrons of cavalry, with William in the middle surrounded by the élite of his knights, so that he could send his orders in all directions, by hand-signal and by shouting. If some ancient historian had described Harold's battle-line, he would have said that rivers dried up at its passing and forest-trees came crash-ing down as it advanced. Enormous forces of Englishmen had come together from all parts of the country, some through their devotion to Harold, all because of their love for their fatherland, which they were determined to defend against these foreign invaders, however wrongly. The land of the Danes, who were their blood-relations, had sent many troops in support. They did not dare to meet William on the level ground, for they considered him a more formidable adversary than the King of the Norwegians. They stationed themselves in a position overlooking him, on a hillside adjacent to the wood through which they had advanced. They immediately dismounted from their horses and all massed densely together on foot. The duke and his men, in no way dismayed by the sharp incline, began to advance slowly up the steep hill.

The awesome baying of trumpets announced the onset of battle on both sides. Eager and brave, the Normans were the first to engage the enemy. Just as in a court of law the speakers for the prosecution open a case of larceny, so here the accusing party was the first to strike a blow. The Norman infantry rushed forward and challenged the English, wounding them and killing them with their missiles. The English resisted strongly, each in his own way. They hurled their javelins and missiles of all sorts, they dealt savage blows with their axes and with stones hafted on wooden handles. You can well imagine how our men were crushed by these weapons, by this massive death-dealing onslaught. Then the knights rode forward, those who had hitherto been in support becoming the first line. Scorning to fight from a distance, they bravely engaged the enemy with their swords. The din of the shouting, from the Normans on this side, from the barbarians on that, could hardly be heard for the clang of their weapons and the groans of the dying. For some time the battle raged fiercely on both sides. The English were helped by the advantage of their higher position, which, massed tightly together, they held without attempting to advance. They also had a great numerical advantage and they kept their ranks very close. What is more, the weapons with which they fought easily cut through shields and other protective armour. With great vigour they held those who dared to attack them hand-to-hand with their swords, and then began to drive them back. Even those who were throwing javelins from a distance were wounded. The Norman infantry turned in flight, terrified by this savage onslaught, and so did the knights from Brittany and the other auxiliaries on the left flank. Almost the whole battle-line of Duke William fell back, a fact which can be admitted without affront to the Normans, that unconquerable race. Even the armies of majestic Rome, which won so many victories on land and sea, occasionally turned in flight, although supported by royal troops, when they learned that their leader was killed, or thought that he was dead. The Normans imagined that their duke had fallen. Their flight was nothing to be ashamed of; instead we should grieve at it, for they thought that they had lost their strong bulwark.

When he saw the greater part of the enemy force moving forward in pursuit, our leader rushed after his retreating troops, blocking those who were running away, bellowing at them and threatening them with his lance. He dragged off his helmet and showed his bared head. 'Look at me!' he shouted. 'I am still alive! With God's help I shall win! What lunacy makes you turn in flight? What retreat is open to you if you run? They will drive you on and slaughter you! You have it in your power to cut them down like a flock of sheep! You are giving up victory and fame which would last for ever! If you keep on, not a single one of you will escape death!' They took new courage from his words. He him- self rode on again at their head. Thundering forward with his sword, he slaugh- tered this enemy people who had merited death by rebelling against him, their king. The Normans dashed back into battle, encircled the thousands who had pursued them and wiped them out in a moment, so that there was not a single survivor.

Reassured in their courage, the Normans attacked the huge army with great violence. Despite the disaster which it had suffered, it seemed as big as ever. The English, who were very sure of themselves, fought with all their might, their great objective being to avoid a breach being made in their line by those who were assailing them. They were so densely massed that the men who were killed could hardly fall to the ground. However, gaps began to appear in their ranks here and there, where the iron weapons of our brave soldiers were having their effect. They were attacked by the men of Le Mans, the Ile-de-France, Brittany and Aquitaine, but the Normans were the bravest of all. An in- experienced young knight from Normandy, Robert, son of Roger of Beaumont, nephew and heir of Count Hugo of Meulan through Hugo's sister Adelina, who was fighting that day for the first time, performed a feat worthy of being remembered for all time. At the head of his battalion, which he was leading on the right flank, he attacked the enemy and laid about him with great courage. Supposing that I wished to do so, which I do not, it would not be possible for me to describe, according to their merit, the remarkable acts of valour performed by various individuals. Even the most fluent writer, and one who had actually been an eye-witness of this battle, would find it difficult to recount each incident in detail. My aim is to hurry on as quickly as possible to the point where I can stop praising Duke William and begin my account of William the King.

The Normans and their allies realized that they could never overcome the vast army of their enemies, all fighting as one man, unless they were prepared to accept very heavy losses. They therefore withdrew, deliberately pretending to turn in flight. They were mindful of the fact that only a short time before their retreat had been turned into success. Now that the barbarians seemed to be on the point of victory, they were filled with great exultation. They shouted to each other and a great cry went up as they hurled insults at our men, threatening to overrun them without more ado. As had happened on the previous occasion, some thousand or more of the English rushed boldly forward, thinking to harass those who were running away. Suddenly the Normans turned their horses, cut off the force which was pursuing them, made a complete circle round them and massacred them to the last man.

Twice the Normans had used this ruse with equal success. Then they made a fierce attack on those who were left. The English battle-line was still terrifying to behold and the Normans had great difficulty in containing it. The fighting which followed was most unusual, for one side continued the attack in a series of charges and individual assaults, while the other stood firm as if rooted to the ground. The English were weakening and suffered heavy losses, as if they were admitting the injustice of their cause by accepting defeat. The Normans shot their arrows, brandished their swords, transfixed the enemy with their spears. The dead, as they tumbled to the ground, showed more sign of motion than the living. The serried mass of their companions prevented those who were lightly wounded from withdrawing, so tightly were they grouped together. Fortune favoured William as it became more and more clear that he would win.

Among those who fought in this battle were Eustace, Count of Boulogne; William, son of Richard, Count of Evreux; Geoffrey, son of Rotrou, Count of Mortagne; William FitzOsbern; Aimeri, governor of Thouars; Walter Giffard; Hugo of Montfort; Raoul of Tosny; Hugo of Grandmesnil; William of Warenne; and a great number of other most famous fighting-men whose names should be recorded in history-books for their warlike deeds. Just as he was wiser than they were, so was William, their duke, more brave. He is to be compared with the leaders of ancient Greece and Rome who are so highly praised in books, and he can justly be set before quite a few of them. He led his forces with great skill, holding them when they turned in flight, giving them courage, sharing their danger. He was more often heard shouting to them to follow him than ordering them to go on ahead. It is abundantly clear that it was the duke's bravery which inspired his soldiers as they advanced and gave them courage. As they stared in astonishment at this terrifying knight-at-arms, a considerable part of the enemy army lost heart long before they were wounded. Three horses were killed under him. Three times he leapt undismayed to the ground and put paid to the man who had slaughtered his horse. That can show you how quick he was in his decisions, how strong he was physically and how steadfast. With savage sword-blows, brooking no delay, he cleft shields, helmets, hauberks. With his own shield he struck a number of the enemy. His soldiers, some of them wounded, took new courage when they saw him fighting on foot. Some, who were weak from loss of blood, leant on their shields and fought on manfully; others, who could do no more, shouted to their comrades and made gestures to them, encouraging them to follow where the duke had led, lest victory should slip out of their hands. William himself helped quite a few to safety.

In the poems which have been written about him Harold is compared with Hector and Turnus. William would have had the courage to meet this Harold in single combat, thus playing Achilles to his Hector and Aeneas to his Turnus. When attacked by fifty adversaries, Tydeus fought them off with a rock: William, who was as nobly-born as Tydeus, would not have feared a thousand. The man who wrote the *Thebaid* and the author of the *Aeneid*, who in their books, as is the way of poets, exaggerate the triumphs of their great heroes, by telling the simple truth about our duke's exploits would have had as great a story to relate and, indeed, a worthier one. What is more, if the striking nature of this theme had brought them inspiration, they would in their smooth numbers have placed him equal with the gods – if only they had lived to write suitable poems about him. My own thin prose which, for the kings who reign hereafter, aims in all humility at recording his piety in worshipping the one true God – He who alone is God from eternity until the end of time and onwards – must now bring to a rapid conclusion the story of this battle which, with justice on his side, he fought so bravely.

As the daylight began to fade the English troops realized that they no longer had the strength to resist the Normans. They knew that they were grievously weakened by the losses which they had sustained, that their king was dead and his brothers with him, and that at their side had perished quite a few of the great leaders of their country. Those who remained were exhausted and at the end of their tether; and they had no one to whom they could look for support. Despite their own losses, the Normans seemed as strong as ever. The longer they fought the stronger they seemed to be; and their onslaught was even fiercer now than it had been at the beginning. In his ferocity the duke would spare no man who offered him resistance. His warlike valour would not lose its edge except in victory. The English turned in flight and made off at full speed, some on the horses which they had seized, others on foot, some along the trackways, most of them through the pathless desert. Bathed in their blood, they struggled to escape, while others dragged themselves to their feet but could not walk a step. Their frantic desire to escape gave new strength to some. Many died where they dropped in the deep recesses of the woods; and even more were discovered by those in pursuit where they had fallen along the trackways. Although the country was unknown to them, the Normans pursued the English relentlessly, cutting the fugitives down from behind and putting the finishing touch to the victory which they had won. Their horses' hoofs took a last toll of the corpses, as they rode over them where they lay.

As they fled some hope of renewing the battle revived in the English, for they took every advantage of a deep gully and a series of ditches. This people, which is descended from the ancient Saxons, the most ferocious of men, has never been slow to cross swords with an enemy. They would not have turned in flight, had it not been in the face of the overwhelming odds. Only a short time before they had crushed with great ease the King of the Norwegians, supported as he was by an enormous army of fierce warriors. When our leader, riding on at the head of his victorious standards, perceived these enemy battalions so unexpectedly drawn up before him, he refused to turn aside or stay his course, although he was under the impression that supporting troops must have come fresh to the fight. Armed only with a broken fragment of his lance, he was more terrible to behold than these men who brandished their long javelins. In a loud voice he forbade Count Eustace to withdraw, although he was turning back with fifty knights and had every intention of sounding the retreat. Eustace was of a different opinion and quietly advised the duke to desist, saying that if he continued to advance he would soon be killed. As he said this, Eustace was struck between the shoulders by a resounding blow, so violent that the blood streamed from his nose and mouth. With the help of his comrades he moved back, looking as if he had not long to live. The duke scorned to show fear or to incur disgrace: he advanced against the enemy and flung them to the ground. Some of the most noble Norman knights fell in this encounter, for the difficult terrain gave them no chance of proving their valour.

Once he had completed his victory, the duke rode back to the battlefield to survey the dead. It was impossible to contemplate them without being moved to pity, although these men who had been slaughtered were most impious: moreover, it is a fine thing and a meritorious action, worthy of great renown, to put an end to the life of a tyrant. The flower of English youth and nobility littered the ground far and wide. At the king's side they found his two brothers. Harold was recognized, not by any insignia which he wore and certainly not from his features, but by certain distinguishing marks. They carried his body to William's camp and it was handed over for burial to William, surnamed Malet. The duke refused to give the corpse to Harold's mother, although she offered an equal weight of gold for the remains of her son whom she loved so much. He fully realized how unseemly it would have been to have accepted gold in exchange in this way. He was quite convinced that it would have been wrong to have allowed Harold to be buried as his mother wished, for as the result of his boundless ambition innumerable men lay dead and uninterred. They said jokingly that his body should be placed there in position to guard the sea-shore and the ocean, which, in his fury, he had till then invested with his arms.

We Normans offer you no insult, Harold: rather we pity you and weep to see your fate, we and the pious Conqueror, who was saddened by your fall. You won such measure of success as you deserved, and then, again as you deserved, you met your death, bathed in your own heart's blood. Now you lie there, in your grave by the sea: by generations yet unborn of English and of Normans you will ever be accursed. So must fall those who in great earthly power seek their own supreme good, who rejoice only when usurping it, who, once that it is seized, strive to retain it by the force of arms. More than that, you were raddled with your brother's blood, fearing as you did that in his greatness he might make your own seem less. Then in mad fury you rushed headlong towards this second fight, so that, while encompassing the downfall of your fatherland, you might endeavour to retain the kingly power. The cataclysm which you caused dragged you down in its wake. You shine no more beneath the crown which you so wrongfully usurped; you sit no longer on the throne to which you proudly climbed. Your last expiring moments proved if it were right or wrong for you to be exalted by this gift made by King Edward as he died. That comet, terror of all kings, which gleamed so bright when you were newly crowned, was but a presage of your own defeat.

the bayeux tapestry

Description of the Tapestry

The Bayeux Tapestry consists of six sections, some say eight, of coarse bleached linen material, joined together to make a strip measuring 230' 10¼" long and varying in width between 19½" and 20½". The joins are disguised by the embroidery and not easy to detect. On this cloth is depicted in coloured wools the story of Harold, from the moment when, as Earl of the East Angles, he said goodbye to King Edward the Confessor in 1063 or 1064, before setting sail from Bosham, until his death at the Battle of Hastings on 14 October 1066 and the flight from the battlefield of the English survivors. The seventy or more incidents are explained by a series of Latin sentences in rustic capitals mixed with semi-uncials, all about 1" high. Along the top runs a border, varying in width from 3" to 4", and portraying animals and birds, with an occasional human figure, nine of the designs representing well known fables, which are closely comparable with those written in French verse by Marie de France and with the collection in Latin prose known to scholars as *LBG* because three of the manuscripts exist in London, Brussels and Göttingen. Along the bottom runs a similar border which, from the beginning of the Battle of Hastings onwards, becomes a welter of human bodies. The Tapestry begins with an upright border of naturalistic scroll-work representing a tree. The upright border with which, in all probability, it originally ended, has long since disappeared and with it an unknown length of the Tapestry.

Wool of eight colours was used in the embroidery: terracotta red, bluish-green, sage-green, dark green, yellow, buff, blue and dark blue. These colours are employed capriciously, but with great effect. The dying of the wools was not uniform, and the colours have faded in varying degrees over the years. When the Tapestry was restored in 1842, machine-spun wool was used to replace parts of the original hand-spun wool; and the harsh colours of these new threads clash with the soft pastel shades of the old ones.

It is thought that the design for the entire sequence of events to be depicted in

the Tapestry was drawn in full detail on the various sections of the linen background by a single master-craftsman of great artistic talent, possibly in charcoal
or perhaps in some more durable medium. He would presumably have received
the most precise directions before he started and maybe as he went along. As
he advanced he may well have returned occasionally to the earlier sections of
his design to make changes here and there, and so keep the story in balance and
in agreement with itself. Whether or not he made a series of rough sketches first
and then copied these on to the linen we shall never know.

The method used by the embroiderers was first to establish each figure by a
line of stem-stitches and outline-stitches, and then to block it in with what is
known as 'laid and couched work'. That is to say, each particular area was filled
in by a series of parallel threads of wool running closely side by side, and these
were then held in place by other holding threads set at right angles to the laid
work and about $\frac{1}{8}''$ apart. The Bayeux Tapestry is thus not a tapestry at all, but
an embroidered hanging. The background is bare linen. It is impossible that
such an immense embroidery could be the work of one person. It has been
suggested that each of the six or eight sections was prepared in a separate work-
shop; but there is no marked variation in the style of the different parts of the
embroidery.

The Tapestry was designed to be hung round a wall, probably in Bayeux
Cathedral. It purpose was to tell the story of the fall of King Harold and the
triumph of William as graphically as possible to an illiterate people. The captions enhanced the understanding of those who could read Latin; no doubt
they also served as running headlines for churchmen who were explaining the
sequence of events to groups of visitors.

It has often been said that the Bayeux Tapestry is unique in that it has sur-
vived, that we have it and that we have nothing else like it. It has been compared
with illustrations in manuscripts of the time, and with the famous bas-reliefs
carved in stone on the architrave of one of the doorways of Modena Cathedral
and outside the great portal of San Zeno in Verona. Mentions of comparable
hangings have been found in more or less contemporary poems and chronicles.
Fragments of not dissimilar embroidery have been preserved from Røn in
Norway, from Skøg in Sweden and from various churches in Iceland. One can
assume that embroidered hangings similar to the Bayeux Tapestry were not un-
common in western Europe in the eleventh and twelfth centuries. It remains true
that nothing comparable has come down to us from the period.

The history of the Tapestry

Where and when the Bayeux Tapestry was made, and who commissioned it, are all matters for conjecture. The opinion generally accepted today, although there are strongly divergent views, is that it was made within living memory of the events which it portrays. The prominence given to Odo, Bishop of Bayeux, half-brother of Duke William (36, 51, 72), and to two men who later became his tenants, Wadard, in Oxfordshire (48–49), and Vital, in Kent (58), has led to the suggestion that it was he who commissioned it. Certain details in the wording, the words AT HESTENGA. CEASTRA in 52 and the crossed Đ for TH in the name GYRĐ in 68, encourage one to think that the workmanship is English, although many scholars refuse to accept this. The case has been put that Bishop Odo commissioned the Tapestry, in England, possibly in Canterbury, where there was a school of artists, that it was first displayed at the dedication of his cathedral in Bayeux in 1077, and that it had been embroidered during the eleven years which preceded that ceremony. It seems possible that certain of the chroniclers listed on pp. 24–31 had seen it, more especially, perhaps, William of Jumièges and William of Poitiers. Any opinion about this depends on the dating of their works and of the Tapestry. It is possible, too, that Robert Wace knew of it. What is certain is that none of them mentions it.

After the dedication ceremony in 1077 there followed a silence of some four hundred years. In 1476, in a manuscript inventory of the possessions of the Cathedral of Notre-Dame in Bayeux, the Tapestry was mentioned specifically for the first time. It is listed there among 'les tentes, tapis, cortines, paremens des autelz et autres draps de saye pour parer le cueur aux festes solennelles trouvés et gardés en le vestiaire de ladicte eglise', and its precise description reads as follows: 'Item une tente tres longue et estroicte de telle a broderie de ymages et escripteaulx, faisans representation du conquest d'Angleterre, laquelle est tendue environ la nef de l'eglise le jour et par les octaves des reliques'. Two hundred and fifty more years passed; and then, in 1724, Antoine Lancelot read to the Académie Royale des Inscriptions et Belles-Lettres in Paris a paper entitled 'Explication d'un monument de Guillaume le Conquérant', in which he announced that he had received from a friend, N. J. Foucault, a sketch of part of this forgotten relic, but that he had not seen it himself and did not even know if it really was a fresco, a series of stained-glass windows, or a tapestry. In 1728 the French antiquarian, Dom Bertrand de Montfaucon, one of the Benedictines of

Saint-Maur, began to take an interest in the discovery and a year later Antoine Benoît was sent at his instance to make a drawing of the Tapestry, which Montfaucon then published in his book *Monuments de la Monarchie française*, Volumes I–II, 1729–30.

During the French Revolution several attempts were made to destroy the Tapestry and to use it for ignoble purposes. In 1803 it was removed to the Musée Napoléon in Paris and there it was exhibited. Napoleon Bonaparte, then First Consul, is said to have studied it closely. A comet appeared in November 1803 and, although it was not Halley's Comet, the omens were considered to be propitious for a new invasion of England, but Napoleon abandoned his plan and early in 1804 the Tapestry was returned to Bayeux. There it has remained ever since, except for a short period during the Franco-Prussian War and again in 1941 during the Second World War. In 1944, after the liberation of France, it was exhibited for four months in the Louvre. It is now on permanent display in a gallery specially designed for it in the former Bishop's Palace in Bayeux.

It is of interest to English readers to learn what part scholars of our own country have played in these affairs. William Stukeley, who had followed with interest the researches of Antoine Lancelot and Dom Bertrand de Montfaucon, was the first Englishman to mention the Tapestry, in his *Paleographia Britannica* of 1746. In 1752 Dr Andrew Ducarel visited Bayeux to examine the Tapestry, which he described in his *Anglo-Norman Antiquities* of 1767, reproducing the drawings made by Antoine Benoît. In 1812 Francis Douce translated the *Recherches sur la Tapisserie représentant la Conquête de l'Angleterre par les Normands* by the Abbé de la Rue and published them with a commentary in *Archaeologia*. Hudson Gurney saw the Tapestry in 1814. In 1818 the Society of Antiquaries sent Charles Stothard to Bayeux to make a complete drawing, which took him three years. Thomas Dibdin went to see the Tapestry in 1818, Dawson Turner in the same year, H. Gally Knight in 1831 and Spencer Smith in 1836. In 1840 it was proposed that an Anglo-French commission should be set up to make a detailed study of it, but nothing came of the project. Since the mid-nineteenth century a great number of Englishmen have written books on the Tapestry, among others J. C. Bruce, F. R. Fowke, C. Dawson, Hilaire Belloc, Eric Maclagan and in 1957 a team led by Sir Frank Stenton. These books are listed in the Select Bibliography on pp. 109–10.

When Dr Ducarel was in Bayeux in 1752, the Tapestry was still being hung round the nave of the cathedral on 1 June and subsequent days each year, and then rolled up and stowed away. In the early nineteenth century it was displayed to visitors by being wound from one roller to another. Those who had the good fortune to see it reported that it was disintegrating rapidly. When he was busy making his copy in the summers of 1818–20, Charles Stothard observed traces of the original drawing with no embroidery left to cover it, empty needle-holes where the design or the lettering had disappeared completely, and here and there fragments of hanging wool. About the same time Dawson Turner said of the Tapestry: 'It is much rubbed at the beginning, torn towards the end, and some portions of it are even missing'. Since then attempts have been made to repair it, notably by Edouard Lambert in 1842. A comparison of the drawings made in 1730 by Antoine Benoît and those made in 1818–20 by Charles Stothard with the photographs of 1873 gives evidence of these fairly modern repairs; and it is not improbable that from time to time similar mending had been found necessary in the later Middle Ages.

The importance of the Tapestry

From what has been said already the great importance of the Bayeux Tapestry is obvious enough.

As a specimen of the craftsmanship of the eleventh century it is unique of its kind. It has been compared stylistically with certain other works of art of the period executed in different media, and, as we have seen, it is true that there still exist fragments of not dissimilar mediaeval embroidery from the Scandinavian countries.

If the Tapestry does indeed date from the period 1066–77, it is one of our earliest authorities for the Battle of Hastings and the invasion which preceded it. If it was made later than 1077, it is still, in all probability, within a generation of the events which it depicts. The Tapestry gives a biased view of those events, but, if the women who made it really were English-speaking, it forms some sort of a link between the two points of view, that of the conquerors and that of the people who were conquered. Harold is presented throughout as the man in high place who broke his solemn oath, and the message is the vengeance of Almighty God upon the perjuror. It could serve no purpose to denigrate Harold in other ways: the more awesome his valour, the more marked his skill as a military leader, the greater must be the glory of the men who destroyed him. From the opening scenes, when Harold says farewell to King Edward in West-minster and rides off to Bosham, until his death in battle and the flight of such of his troops as are left alive, the story which the Tapestry tells is linear and consecutive. On the other hand, in its details the narrative is selective: there is no mention, for example, of the invasion of Harold Hardraada or of the Battle of Stamford Bridge.

As a sustained work of art the Bayeux Tapestry is again unique of its kind. The original draftsmanship is spirited in the extreme. The facial expressions, most of them in profile, are strongly marked, there is throughout immense vigour of action, and the vitality of all the characters portrayed is most striking. This is true of almost all the scenes: Harold riding with his hawk and his dogs on his way to Bosham (2), William's messengers galloping to Beaurain (12–13), the look-out perched in a tree outside William's palace in Rouen (13), William and Harold setting off on their expedition against the Bretons (19–20), Harold pulling two Norman soldiers out of the quicksands of the River Couesnon (20–21), Conan escaping from the castle of Dol by sliding down a rope (22); but it is most true of the battle-scenes towards the end of the Tapestry. The persons depicted gesticulate with their hands to express their intentions and their emotions, e.g. Harold visiting King Edward in Westminster after his return from Normandy (29–30), the English crowds watching Halley's Comet (34). An attempt is made to depict the different hair-styles of the English and the Normans, the former wearing their hair quite thick on the nape of the neck and the latter being bare almost up to the crown of the head. The English wear thin moustaches, but the Normans are clean-shaven. Much use is made of stylized trees. The interior of buildings is shown, with one or more of the exterior sides brought round to stand square instead of sideways and in perspective, in which case they would, of course, be invisible, e.g. King Edwards' palace in Westminster (1). All the pictures, except the frenzied battle-scenes, give a most unusual sense of space, for the linen back-cloth is left bare. In this the Tapestry differs fundamentally from contemporary miniatures and illuminated initials, in which the background is usually crowded in with gold-leaf work, filigree designs in water colour and cramping detail of one sort and another. It has been said that the Tapestry lacks perspective, but this is not true: figures vary in size, the inside legs of humans, horses and dogs are shaded to give depth, the folds of garments are shown carefully. Admittedly the medium is not an easy one; and there is inevitably a certain stiffness in the finished figures. The women who outlined the cartoons with their stem-stitches, and then filled them in with their parallel threads of wool, were, however, past-mistresses in their craft. The greatest challenge to their skill was perhaps the wooden sides of the ships, and then the chain-mail hauberks of the fighting-men, for they found it virtually impossible to make these three-dimensional. The borders along the top and the bottom begin by being representations of grotesque animals, fables, country scenes, the constellations and other stock motifs, taken perhaps from the model-books of the time if such already existed, but as the story moves to its climax the lower border becomes a running commentary on the Battle of Hastings, with archers in action, a congeries of dead bodies, lopped-off limbs, discarded weapons and corpses which are being stripped. In all this the detail is extraordinary, and as one moves from scene to scene the sense of effort and activity is most striking. Perhaps the best way to appreciate the Tapestry is to take one incident and study it with close attention; as against this the all-over effect is one of dynamic movement. When the designs on the borders are included, there are said to be 626 human figures, 190 horses and mules, 506 other animals, 37 ships, 33 buildings and 37 trees or groups of trees.

Finally, the Bayeux Tapestry is a remarkable social document. There is first the whole range of men's civilian dress, from King Edward the Confessor sitting in full regalia on his throne in Westminster Palace (1) to Turold's be-trousered groom, if that is who the dwarf really is (11), from the watchman in his sombre tunic and rough stockings in the tree outside William's castle in Rouen (13) to Duke William himself riding out to meet Count Guy and the captive Harold, wrapped in his embroidered cloak and with his square tie-ends blowing in the wind (15); mantles, riding-cloaks, robes, knee-length tunics, breeches, trousers, hose, shoes. There are only four women in the Tapestry, Queen Edith, with a female attendant, at her husband's bedside as he dies (32), the mysterious Ælfgyva and her priest (18), and the Englishwoman who emerges with her son from their house near Hastings as the ravaging Normans set light to the roof (53): all are wrapped in robes, which reach the ground in the last two pictures, all have kerchiefs round their hair, and the woman in 53 has long hanging sleeves. There are many priests, usually in lay clothes, but always clearly marked with the tonsure. The churchman depicted in most detail is Archbishop Stigand, substituted as a propaganda device for Ealdred of York, at Harold's coronation, bare-headed but wearing a chasuble, an alb and a stole, with a maniple in his left hand (33). Immediately before the coronation of Harold (33) come the death and burial of Edward (32 and 31), curiously enough in inverse order. There are two mealtime scenes, the one showing Duke William and his half-brother, Robert of Mortain, eating soon after their arrival in Hastings (50), with William's other half-brother, Bishop Odo, blessing the food (50), and before that the food being prepared in a field-kitchen (49), and before that again the cattle being rounded up and slaughtered (48). This is balanced in some small degree by the scene of Harold and his men eating and drinking in his house in Bosham before they set out for their ill-fated Channel trip (3–4). In all, as we have seen, there are 33 buildings in the Tapestry, and these range from King Edward's palace in Westminster (1), and the castles in Rennes (23), Dinan (24) and Bayeux (26), to the church in Bosham (3) and the one-storeyed hovels of the English peasants whose cattle have been seized by the foragers (48–49). In parts of the borders there are extremely interesting genre scenes of rural life: the ploughman, sower, harrower and slinger (10–12); the huntsman on foot and the one on horseback (13–14). In 52 we see a fortified mound being thrown up by William's troops at Hastings. There are then the ships, 37 of them. First Harold crosses the Channel to Ponthieu (4–7), then he sails back again to England (27–28). News of King Edward's death and of Harold's coronation is brought to William in an English ship (35), and almost immediately the Normans begin to build their invasion fleet, a long and difficult process which we witness in full detail, from the chopping down of the trees and the smoothing of the planks (37), the work with planes, augurs and adzes (38), the launching of the vessels (38–39), the carrying on board of arms, armour and barrels of wine, but no food, as far as we can see (40–41), and then the embarkation of the troops and their horses (41–42). There remain the scenes of fighting and the evidence which they afford of the military tactics of the time, and of the arms and armour used by the combatants. The first fighting-men whom we see are the knights brought by Count Guy to seize Harold and bring him captive to Beaurain (7–8). A short time afterwards William's two messengers arrive at full gallop, lances at the level, shields on their left upper arms (12–13). In 19–20 Duke William and Earl Harold set off for their joint campaign in Brittany, and from the episodes which follow we can learn a vast amount about contemporary warfare (19–26): chain-mail hauberks, conical helmets with heavy nasals, lances, pennants, high-bowed saddles, stirrups, swords and scabbards, kite-shaped shields with their distinctive devices, siege-warfare and the use of fire-buckets, unprotected warhorses. In 47 the newly-landed invaders ride at full speed towards Hastings, their heads bare, but wearing their hauberks and carry-ing their lances and their shields. The Battle of Hastings begins in 54, and from there it continues until the end of the Tapestry (54–80). It is at once the central theme and the dramatic climax of the story which the Tapestry has to tell, and a third of the embroidered pictures are devoted to it. From 65 onwards the lower border is a running commentary, a commentary running with blood, on the scenes of death and destruction depicted above. Each of the twenty-six scenes devoted to the battle has much to teach us. The most poignant episode by far is the death of King Harold (77–78): HIC HAROLD REX INTER-FECTVS EST. If, as has been suggested, Harold really is depicted twice in this scene, then it is true that in 77 he seems to be pulling an arrow from his right eye. In 78, which is part of the same picture, he has no shield or javelin, he is wielding a huge single-bladed axe, and he is being struck down with a sword by a Norman knight on horseback.

The Plates

The problems of reproducing the Tapestry are severe. The keepers are naturally reluctant to allow it to be removed from its display casing because of its fragility. It has, therefore, to be photographed *in situ*, preferably with the glass removed, which in itself is a major operation. Even then the difficulties of perspective remain. The Tapestry is a continuous length and any worthwhile reproduction must show it as unbroken as possible. In the Gallery it turns several curved corners so that the photographer must choose his point of view with particular care to make his transparencies butt up into a seemingly continuous whole. He has the additional complication of avoiding breaks in the centre of important scenes. Inevitably some of the reproductions show the curved edges and slight changes of scale caused by the curved support of the Tapestry itself. The photographer, Michael Holford, is to be congratulated on producing such an even and regular set of eighty transparencies.

The reproduction here has aimed at continuous verisimilitude. The edges of the transparencies are brought together to give an appearance of continuity without attempting to join them by artificial means. Sufficient overlap has been allowed to enable the reader to make the visual connection where breaks occur from page to page. In five places it has been necessary to repeat portions in order to maintain the flow, and this was thought preferable to leaving blanks. They are numbers 24, 39, 62, 71 and part of 72, and are clearly marked in the captions.

the plates

1. KING EDWARD. WHERE HAROLD,

3. BOSHAM. THE CHURCH.

. VX: ANGLORVM: ET SVI MILITES: EQVITANT: AD BOS

2. THE EARL OF THE ENGLISH, AND HIS KNIGHTS ARE RIDING TO

HIC HAROLD: MARE NAVIGAVIT: ET VE

4. HERE HAROLD HAS CROSSED THE SEA AND

VE: LIS: VENTO: PLENIS: VE=
=NIT: INTE: RR: A:
VVIOONIS
COMITIS

5. WITH HIS SAILS FULL OF WIND HAS COME TO THE TERRITORY OF
COUNT GUY.

D: HIC: APPREHENDIT: VVIDO: HAROLD: ET

7. HERE GUY HAS CAPTURED HAROLD AND

6. HAROLD.

8. LED HIM OFF TO BEAURAIN AND THERE

9. HELD HIM PRISONER.   WHERE

11. WHERE DUKE WILLIAM'S ENVOYS HAVE COME TO
TUROLD.

10. HAROLD AND GUY ARE TALKING TOGETHER.

12. GUY.   WILLIAM'S ENVOYS.

13. HERE A MESSENGER HAS COME TO DUKE WILLIAM.

15. WILLIAM, DUKE OF THE NORMANS.

14. HERE GUY HAS TAKEN HAROLD TO

16. HERE DUKE WILLIAM WITH HAROLD

17. HAS COME TO HIS PALACE.

19. AND HIS ARMY HAVE COME TO THE MONT SAINT-MICHEL

18. WHERE A CHURCHMAN AND AELFGYVA . . . HERE DUKE WILLIAM

20. AND HERE THEY HAVE CROSSED THE RIVER COUESNON
HERE EARL HAROLD WAS DRAGGING THEM OUT OF THE QUICKSAND.

MEN : COSNONIS : ET VENERVNT   AD DOL : ET CO
VX : TRAHEBAT : EOS :
NA

21. COUESNON AND COME TO DOL, AND CONAN
(WAS DRAGGING THEM)

IT :   HIC MILITES   VVILLELMI : DVCIS : PVG
RED   NES

23. HERE DUKE WILLIAM'S KNIGHTS ARE FIGHTING
RENNES.

22. HAS TURNED IN FLIGHT.

24. AGAINST THE MEN OF DINAN, AND

24 *bis*. AGAINST THE MEN OF DINAN, AND

26. HERE WILLIAM HAS COME TO BAYEUX,

25. CONAN HAS HANDED OVER THE KEYS. HERE WILLIAM HAS GIVEN HAROLD ARMS.

27. WHERE HAROLD MADE AN OATH TO DUKE WILLIAM. HERE EARL HAROLD

28. HAS RETURNED

30. TO EDWARD THE KING.   HERE

AD ANGLICAM : TERRAM : ET VENIT : AD : ED

29. TO ENGLAND AND HAS COME

TUR : CORPVS : EADWARDI : REGIS : AD : ECCLESIAM : S PETRI A

31. KING EDWARD'S BODY IS BEING CARRIED TO THE CHURCH OF SAINT PETER

M:SCI APLI

hIC EADWARDVS:REX INLECTO:ALLOQVIT:FIDE:LES: hIC DEDE CORO

ET hIC: DEFVNCTVS EST

32. THE APOSTLE. HERE KING EDWARD, IN BED, IS ADDRESSING HIS LIEGEMEN, AND HERE HE IS DEAD. HERE THEY HAVE GIVEN

ISTI MIRANT STELLA

HAROLD

34. THESE PEOPLE ARE MARVELLING AT THE STAR. HAROLD.

33. THE KING'S CROWN TO HAROLD.   HERE SITS HAROLD, KING
    ARCHBISHOP STIGANT.   OF THE ENGLISH.

35. HERE AN ENGLISH SHIP

HIC·WILLELM
NAVES·EDI

·VENIT·INTER
WILLELMI·DV

RAM
CIS

36. HAS COME TO DUKE WILLIAM'S TERRITORY.   HERE DUKE WILLIAM

37. HAS ORDERED SHIPS TO BE BUILT.

39. HERE THEY ARE DRAGGING THE SHIPS TO THE SEA.

TRAHVNT:NAVES:ADMARE:

39 *bis*. THEY ARE DRAGGING THE SHIPS TO THE SEA.

VES:ETHIC
VNT:CARRVM
INO:ETARMIS:
+HIC:VVILLELM:DVX   INMAG

41. AND HERE THEY ARE PULLING A CART WITH WINE AND ARMS.
HERE DUKE WILLIAM IN A BIG

40. THESE MEN ARE CARRYING ARMS TO THE SHIPS.

42. SHIP

43. HAS CROSSED OVER THE SEA

45. HERE THE HORSES ARE DISEMBARKING

44. AND HAS COME TO PEVENSEY.

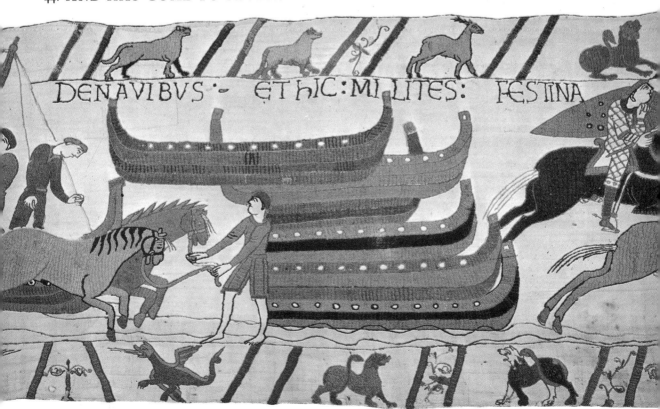

46. FROM THE SHIPS AND HERE THE KNIGHTS HAVE HURRIED OFF

47. TO HASTINGS SO THAT THEY MIGHT FORAGE FOR FOOD.

49. HERE THE MEAT IS BEING COOKED AND HERE THE SERVANTS HAVE SERVED IT.

HIC:EST:VVADARD:

48. THIS IS WADARD.

HIC FECERVN: PRANDIVM:

ET HIC EPISCOPVS:CIBV:E
POTV: BE NE DIC IT:

50. HERE THEY HAVE HAD THEIR MEAL, AND HERE THE BISHOP IS
BLESSING THE FOOD AND DRINK.

ET ODO:EPS: ROTBERT: ISTE:IVSSIT: VT FO D

WILLELM:

51. BISHOP ODO. WILLIAM. ROBERT. THIS MAN HAS GIVEN THE
ORDER THAT

IC:NVNTIATVM EST: hIC DOMVS:IN
VILLELM DE HAROLD: CENDITVR:

53. NEWS CONCERNING HAROLD HAS BEEN BROUGHT TO WILLIAM.
HERE A HOUSE IS BEING BURNT.

TVR:CASTELLVM:AͰHESTENGᴬ CEASTRA HIC: WILI

52. A FORTIFICATION SHOULD BE DUG AT HASTINGS.   THE CAMP.   HERE

HIC:MILITES:EXIERVNT:DEhESTENGA

54. HERE THE KNIGHTS HAVE SET OUT FROM HASTINGS

55. AND HAVE REACHED

57. THE KING.   HERE DUKE WILLIAM IS ASKING

AD PRELIVM: CON TRA: HAROL DV

56. THE BATTLE AGAINST HAROLD

ITAL: SIVI DISSET EXER CI TV

HAROLDI

58. VITAL IF HE HAS SEEN HAROLD'S ARMY.

59. THIS MAN IS GIVING NEWS OF DUKE WILLIAM'S

61. IS EXHORTING HIS KNIGHTS TO PREPARE

HAROLDVM DEEXERCITV   HIC WILLELM:DVX

60. ARMY TO KING HAROLD.   HERE DUKE WILLIAM

ENSE VIRILITER   ETSA

62. THEMSELVES MANFULLY AND

62 *bis*. THEMSELVES MANFULLY AND

64. THE ARMY OF THE ENGLISH.

63. PRUDENTLY FOR THE BATTLE AGAINST

66.

LEVVINE   ET GYRÐ FRATRES HA

68. LEOFWINE AND GYRTH, THE BROTHERS OF HAROLD

67. HERE HAVE FALLEN

69. THE KING.   HERE HAVE FALLEN

70. SIDE BY SIDE THE ENGLISH AND THE FRENCH IN

71 *bis*. IN THE BATTLE.   HERE ODO

71. THE BATTLE.   HERE ODO

72. THE BISHOP, HOLDING A CLUB, IS URGING ON THE YOUNG SOLDIERS.
HERE IS WILLIAM.

EUSTACE.

73. IS URGING ON THE YOUNG SOLDIERS. HERE IS DUKE WILLIAM.

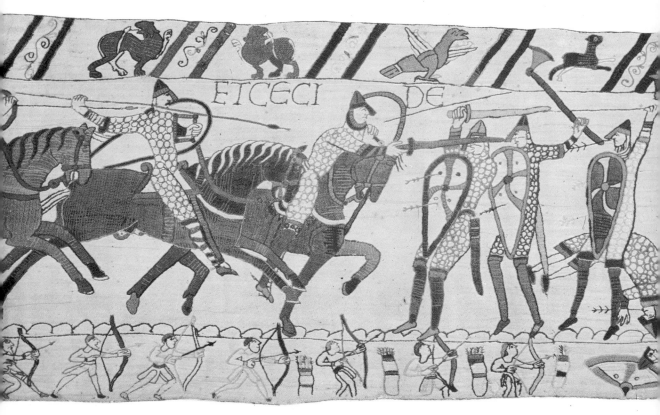

75. AND THOSE HAVE FALLEN

74. THE FRENCH ARE FIGHTING,

76. WHO WERE WITH HAROLD.

77. HERE KING HAROLD

79. AND THE ENGLISH HAVE TURNED IN FLIGHT.

INTERFEC TVS:EST

E

78. HAS BEEN KILLED

select bibliography

PRIME SOURCES

The Lives of Edward the Confessor, edited by H. R. Luard, Rolls Series, London, 1858.

The Anglo-Saxon Chronicle, best read, in English translation, in *English Historical Documents*, Volume II, 1042-1189, edited by David C. Douglas and George W. Greenaway, London, 1953, pp. 120-146.

Guillaume de Jumièges, Gesta Normannorum Ducum, édition critique par Jean Marx, *Société de l'Histoire de Normandie*, Rouen and Paris, 1914.

Guillaume de Poitiers, Histoire de Guillaume le Conquérant, éditée et traduite par Raymonde Foreville, *Les Classiques de l'Histoire de France au Moyen Age*, Paris, 1952.

The Carmen de Hastingae Proelio of Guy Bishop of Amiens, edited by Catherine Morton and Hope Muntz, *Oxford Medieval Texts*, 1972.

Florentii Wigorniensis [Florence of Worcester] *monachi Chronicon ex Chronicis*, edited by B. Thorpe, *Publications of the English Historical Society*, London, 2 volumes, 1848-49.

Gesta Regum Anglorum, by William of Malmesbury, edited by William Stubbs, Rolls Series, London, 2 volumes, 1887-89.

Henrici Archidiaconi Huntendunensis [Henry of Huntingdon] *Historia Anglorum*, edited by Thomas Arnold, Rolls Series, London, 1879.

Orderici Vitalis Historiae Ecclesiasticae libri tredecim, édités par Auguste le Prevost, *Société de l'Histoire de France*, Paris, 5 volumes, 1838-55.

Le roman de Rou de Wace, publié par A. J. Holden, *Société des Anciens Textes Français*, Paris, 2 volumes, 1970-71.

REPRODUCTIONS OF THE BAYEUX TAPESTRY AND BOOKS ABOUT IT

1856: J. C. Bruce, *The Bayeux Tapestry elucidated*, London. [Discussion, pp. 1-166; coloured frontispiece and 16 coloured plates from Charles Stothard's 1818-20 drawings].

1875: F. R. Fowke, *The Bayeux Tapestry*, London. [Discussion; full black-and-white reproduction on autotype plates].

1898: F. R. Fowke, *The Bayeux Tapestry. A history and description*, Bohn's Antiquarian Library, London. [Discussion, pp. 1-139; full black-and-white photographic reproduction].

1907: C. Dawson, *The 'Restorations' of the Bayeux Tapestry*, London. [Discussion, 14pp.].

1914: Hilaire Belloc, *The book of the Bayeux Tapestry*, London. [Discussion, pp. v-xviii; full coloured photographic reproduction, with commentary].

1919: A. Levé, *La Tapisserie de la reine Mathilde, dite la Tapisserie de Bayeux*, Paris. [Discussion, pp. 1-212; full black-and-white photographic reproduction bound in, with frontispiece].

1923: Roger S. Loomis, 'The origin and date of the Bayeux Embroidery', article in *The Art Bulletin,* Vol. VI, No. 1, 4 pp.

1934: H. Chefneux, 'Les fables dans la Tapisserie de Bayeux', two articles in *Romania,* Vol. LX, pp. 1–35, 153–194. [Discussion, with 10 line drawings of parts of the border].

1943: Sir Eric Maclagan, *The Bayeux Tapestry,* King Penguin. [Discussion, pp. 5–32; full black-and-white photographic reproduction + 8 coloured plates].

1946: J. Verrier, *La Broderie de Bayeux, dite Tapisserie de la Reine Mathilde,* Paris. [Discussion, pp. I–IV; full black-and-white photographic reproduction + 8 coloured plates].

1953: David C. Douglas and George W. Greenaway, *English Historical Documents 1042–1189,* London. [Discussion, pp. 232–238; full black-and-white photographic reproduction, pp. 239–278].

1958: Sir Frank Stenton, Simone Bertrand, George Wingfield Digby, Charles H. Gibbs-Smith, Sir James Mann, John L. Nevinson and Francis Wormald, *The Bayeux Tapestry. A Comprehensive Survey,* Phaidon. [Discussion, pp. 9–88, 162–182; 150 photographic reproductions, including 14 in colour].

Set in 13 point Poliphilus leaded 1 point
with Libra type for display.
Text printed photo-litho by Mackays of Chatham Ltd,
transparencies by Michael Holford
printed in four colours by photo-litho
by Jolly & Barber Ltd.
Bound by Mackays of Chatham Ltd
using Wintex cloth and Opal Tyvek paper.